JOYCE CAIRNS *WAR TOURIST*

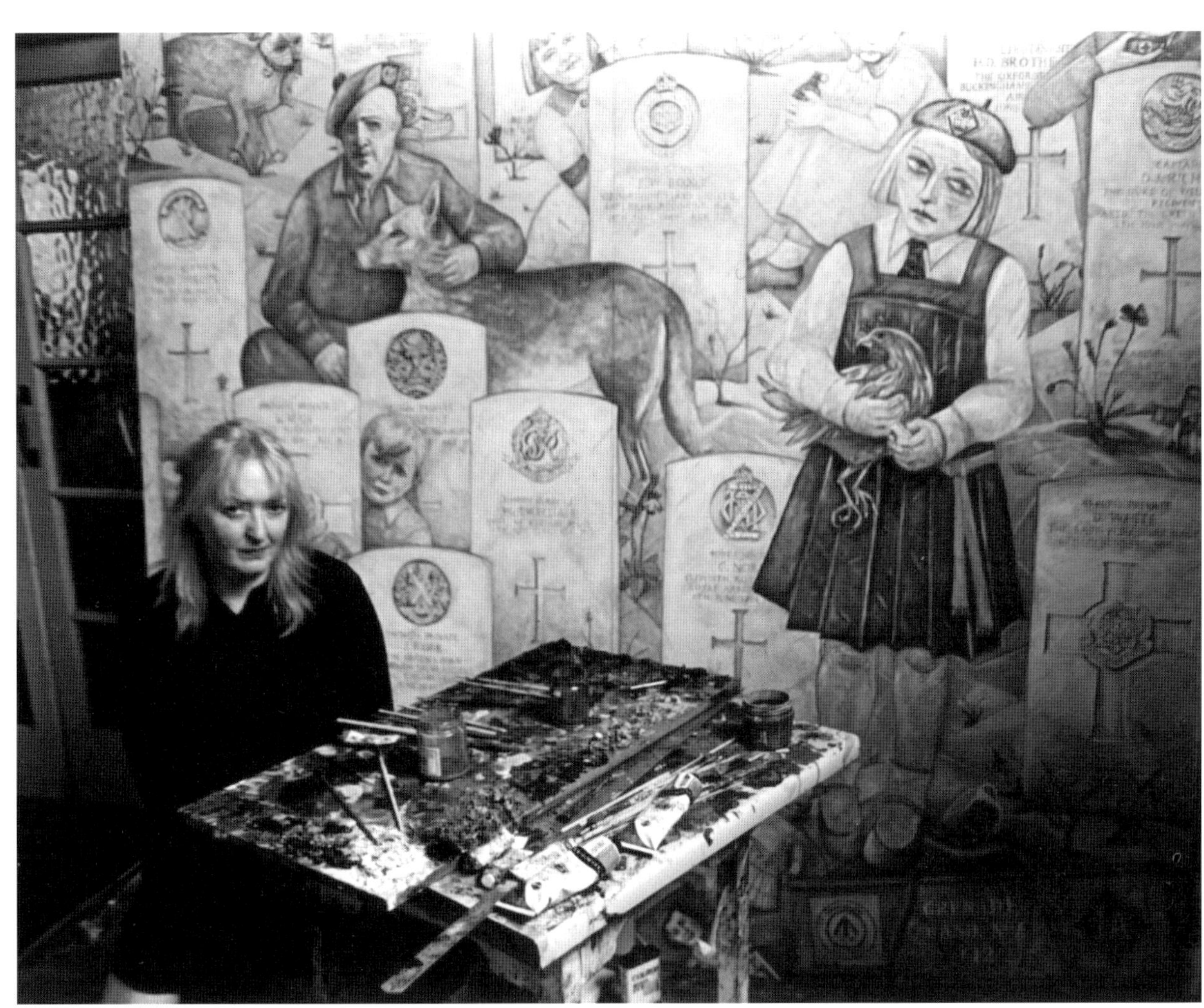

JOYCE CAIRNS *WAR TOURIST*

An illustrated anthology
edited by

ARTHUR WATSON

Aberdeen Art Gallery

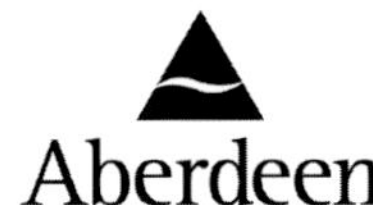

Aberdeen Asset Management PLC
is proud to support the publication of this book.

COVER: *Shoes from Majdanek*, 2002–05
(Detail. See PLATE TWENTY–FOUR, p.103)

INSIDE COVER: *In Flanders Fields*, 2005
(Detail. See PLATE TWELVE, p.73)

FRONTISPIECE: Joyce Cairns in her studio
Photo © 2005 Alan Young

Published in the United Kingdom by
Aberdeen City Council in 2006
for the exhibition
War Tourist Joyce Cairns
11 February to 8 April 2006
Aberdeen Art Gallery
Schoolhill, Aberdeen
Supported by the Scottish Arts Council
National Lottery Fund

ISBN 0 900017 65 1

Directed and edited by
Arthur Watson

Designed and typeset by
Donald Addison

Photography of the artist's works
© 2005 Stuart Johnstone, unless otherwise stated

Printed and bound by
Inglis Allen (UK) Ltd
Kirkcaldy

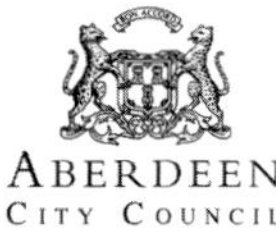

ABERDEEN
CITY COUNCIL

CONTENTS

To my Father and Mother

LIST OF PLATES

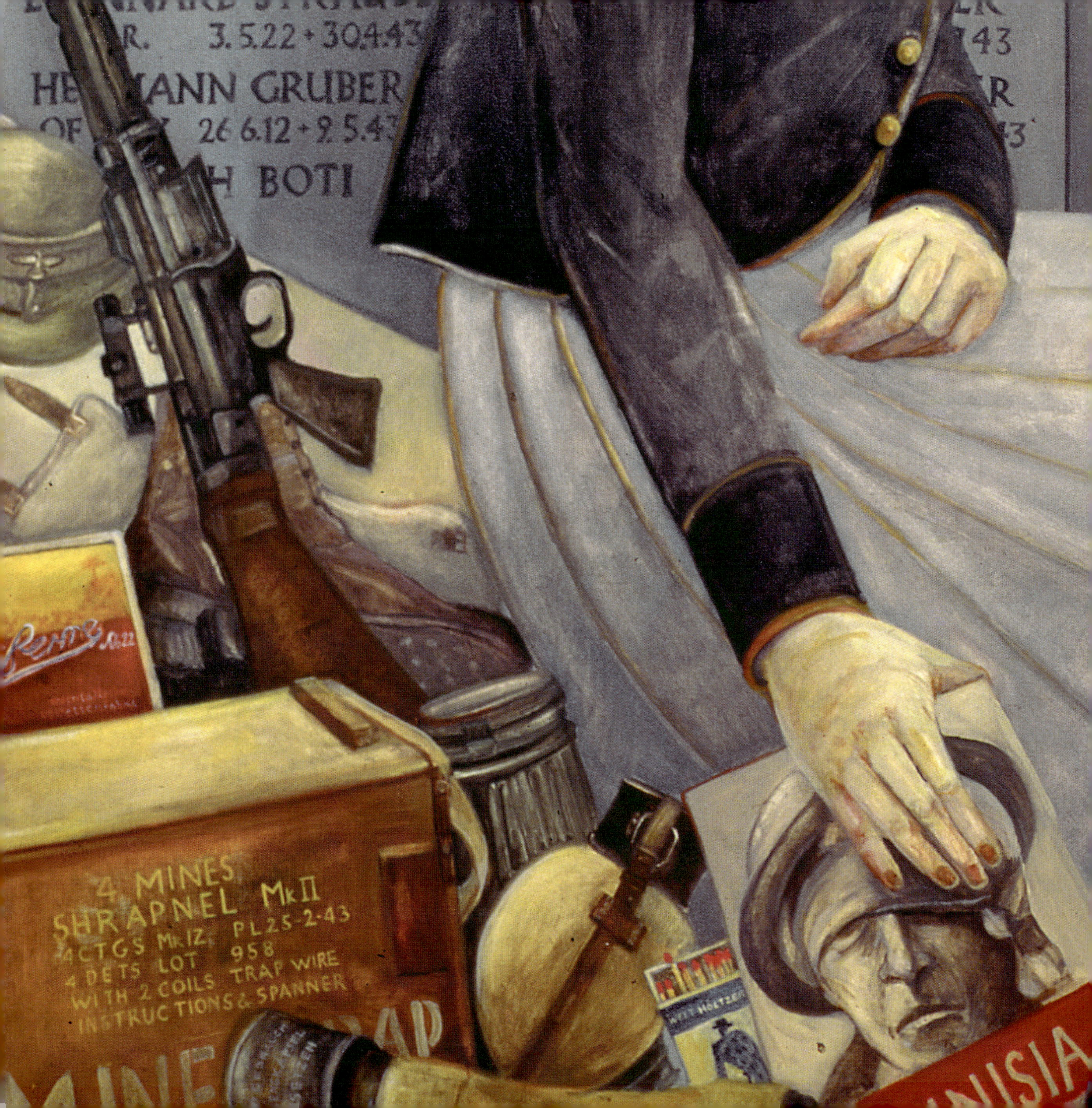
3.5.22 + 30.4.43
GRUBER
26.6.12 + 9.5.43
BOTI
4 MINES
SHRAPNEL MkII
4 CTGS MkIZ PL25-2-43
4 DETS LOT 958
WITH 2 COILS TRAP WIRE
INSTRUCTIONS & SPANNER

FOREWORD

Jennifer Melville

IN THIS LARGE AND IMPRESSIVE BODY OF WORK, Scottish artist Joyce Cairns offers both a deeply personal exploration of her family's experience of war and makes comment on the cruelties and absurdities of war in general. Cairns makes these comments on a grand scale, but gives visual and emotional impact to her paintings by depicting tiny objects, photographs, mementoes and possessions. Through her detailed recording of such individually insignificant artefacts, she builds a story showing how the minutiae of war can reveal the significance of the individual and how, through mere mementoes, a life can be recalled and the contribution of even just one person to a global conflict chronicled.

Joyce Cairns was born in Edinburgh in 1947. After studying in Aberdeen and at the Royal College of Art in London she was awarded a fellowship at Gloucestershire College of Art & Design in Cheltenham. This was followed by a further period of study at Goldsmith's College, University of London. In 1976 she returned to Scotland, taking up a post as lecturer at Gray's School of Art in Aberdeen. Her richly coloured, complex paintings were widely appreciated and Cairns became a highly regarded member of the Scottish art community. In 1985 this culminated in her election to the Royal Scottish Academy. She continued to play an important role in the Aberdeen art world and from 1985–88 served as the first woman President of the Aberdeen Artists' Society.

In 2004 Joyce Cairns decided to take early retirement from Gray's School of Art in order to devote herself to painting full time and to complete a body of work that had increasingly absorbed her. Cairns' work had always been deeply personal and largely autobiographical. In it she combined intense, dreamlike visions with the unique environment of the village of Footdee, in the harbour area of Aberdeen, where she still lives. Ironically, it was to be her exploration of her own past that eventually led her to move away from depicting the world around her and to turn instead to the subject of war. It is this body of work that is discussed in this volume.

Although born after the end of the Second World War, Joyce Cairns was aware that her family's personal experience of this conflict had affected her own life profoundly. Her father, a Queen's Own Cameron Highlander, had seen active service in North Africa and in Europe. Meanwhile the family lived in North East Scotland, where before the War Cairns' father had been headmaster at Cawdor School. Isolated from her own family and with her husband absent for long periods, although distanced from events, the war impacted on her mother too. It was her mother's death many years later that prompted Cairns to explore her parents' past and particularly their experience of war, which during their lifetimes had rarely been discussed. From what began as a very personal exploration of how war affected her family, Cairns moved on to tackle the subject of war in general. She made pilgrimages as a 'war tourist', retracing her father's steps in Normandy and Tunisia. She then visited concentration camps in Germany, Austria and Poland, an upsetting but cathartic experience which enabled her to begin to address her own deeply felt beliefs about war.

In this book three different writers examine Joyce Cairns as a war artist from different viewpoints. In his essay, entitled WITNESSING AND WARNING, art historian Bill Hare shows how her war paintings link with the earlier phases of Cairns' art. He also explains how her interpretation of war is essentially a female one. Through her father's story Cairns recognises individual heroic actions but her stance is fundamentally anti-war; the purpose of her art, he explains, is to rage against the madness, suffering and 'epic tragedy' brought about by such conflicts. As a military historian, Stuart Allan focuses on the social implications of war, showing how long service overseas could cause a damaging dislocation that often affected entire families and could last far longer than the conflict itself. Sandy Moffat looks at the work from an artist's point of view. He questions the morality of turning war into art but concludes that it is a legitimate and worthy subject for all art forms. He then shows how Cairns' war works place her in a long tradition of Scottish artists and poets who have similarly been inspired. He also finds links with her contemporaries, such as Paula Rego. In Rego's now famous painting *War* (Tate) a menagerie of marionettes, some sporting Donnie Darko–style animal masks, symbolise the artist's belief in the lunacy of the war in Iraq. This principle and aesthetic is echoed in Cairns' painting *Irma*. To these essays Cairns herself adds her own explanation of how each work came about and her subsequent, almost obsessional, search to rediscover her father's past.

Joyce Cairns' paintings are essentially northern. They are inspired by Expressionist art, in which form and colour disturb and upset. Cairns' images of her mother's anguish recall the paintings of Edvard Munch. She couples war and death with elements of the macabre, as did her German antecedents, Albrecht Altdorfer, Otto Dix, Max Beckmann and Emil Nolde. With Nolde, Edvard Munch and John Bellany she can at times share their taste for fiery, intense and emotive colour, here most evident in the painting entitled *War Games*. However for most artists, such as Picasso, who live and continue to paint during wartime, the zeitgeist pervades their work, which takes on the sobriety of the war, the camouflage colours of the age. Here we can see this overall sombre quality in many of Cairns' paintings, so that some of them, for example, *Normandy War Graves*, take on the effect of a faded photograph or a distant memory.

This powerful body of work resonates on many levels, bringing together several threads of Joyce Cairns' life and deepest thoughts. Her paintings make noble comment on the cruelties of war and the absurdities of modern life. Through them she shows how such momentous events affect all of us, especially those families for whom war may be an unspoken but life-changing event.

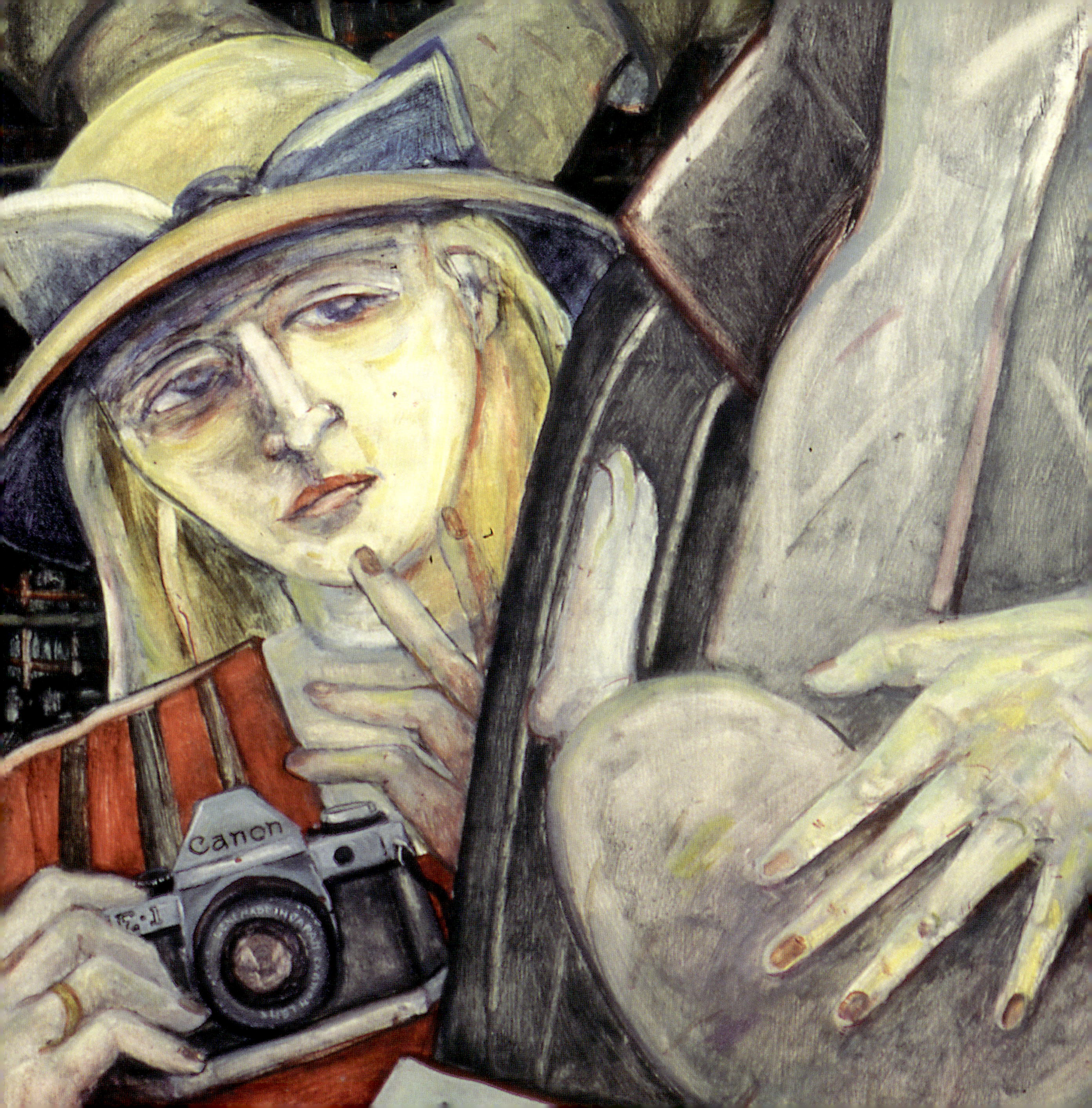
Canon

WAR TOURIST, AN INTRODUCTION

Joyce Cairns

ALTHOUGH CUSTOMARILY SEEN FROM A MALE PERSPECTIVE, war has also indelibly marked wives and mothers as well as their children. In 1984 I witnessed the anniversary ceremonies for the liberation of Rennes. Realising that my father had fought in France, I became increasingly focused on areas in which my essentially female response to his war could be gauged.

Over the past ten years my curiosity about 'my father's war' led to extensive reading and travel. I followed the route of the 1st Army in Tunisia, where my father, a Cameron Highlander, was awarded the MBE, then on to Normandy, where he was with the 3rd Infantry and mentioned in despatches. Other investigative tours have taken me to Germany, Austria and the Czech Republic as well as to the concentration camps and ghettos of Poland. Added stimulus came from regular visits to First World War battlefields in France and Belgium, evidenced by some three thousand photographs.

When I started this project in 1995 I had no idea that it would take the best part of ten years to bring to any sort of conclusion. This book and accompanying exhibition are not intended, nor could they ever be, a full history of major conflict in the twentieth century; rather my response is like that of a tourist as I dip in and out of locations and periods only making work when I discover that crucial emotional link.

Everything I write about family memories and my father's war is from a personal perspective and although I know these stories to be true they cannot always be backed up by factual information so long after the event. As my parents' generation, within the family, are now dead, my questions remain unanswered with them as discreetly silent in death as they had been in life. I had hoped that my brothers and sisters would be able to fill in some of the gaps, but the three born before the war did not wish to relive what was, for them, a harrowing time and my younger brother, to whom my father confided some of his war experiences, felt that the past should remain buried. My only tangible links to that past are through inherited objects and how I wish that they at least could speak to me now.

In the paintings I mix past with present; artefacts which have been seen as treasured objects in museums are conceptually removed and returned to the field of battle or introduced into the domestic environment, a constant reminder of the ugliness and devastation of war. In many of the works my own dominant figure is the 'War Tourist' epitomising compassion, loneliness, despair, terror, pain or even death.

These painted reconstructions are memorials for three generations, friend and foe, who were lost on all fronts in both world wars and in all subsequent conflicts.

Throughout this project I have attempted to explore different forms of pictorial space. My early student works were influenced by the hierarchy, symmetry and flat iconic format of Byzantine and pre-Renaissance painting, particularly Cimabue. In 1972 I was selected by The Royal College of Art to paint a room-size mural on the theme: *The King is Dead, Long Live the King*, for the exhibition MONARCHY 1000 to be held in the Octagon in Bath. This was at the time an ideal commission, given my interest in symbolism, myth and mediaeval aesthetics. The room was 18ft x 13ft x 9ft and the work was painted in London on panels before being transported and re-assembled in Bath. This was my first real experience of thoroughly researching the subject in preparation for painting and my first opportunity to work on such a grand scale.

Planning these large compositions is akin to solving a jigsaw puzzle but with many different alternatives, not only in the choice of images and objects, but also in regard to the spatial arrangement, colour and tonality. Selection is rarely easy. The initial drawing may only suggest the complexity and detail of the finished painting but once the idea is established through drawing I transfer it onto tracing paper, allowing me more freedom to move images around within the composition. I usually work on a grid, exploring the tension and geometry of the positive and negative shapes, as well as easing the process of enlargement to the proportionally gridded panel. Once the skeletal design and the main elements are established on the panels, I add further refinements and layers of detail at this larger scale. The composition is, therefore, fully realised as a detailed drawing before painting begins. I have always worked on board, never canvas, as I prefer a hard smooth ground. Thinned oil paint is applied in washes allowing the initial drawing (and sometimes part of the grid) to show through with the brush marks from the initial priming contributing to the surface quality, while elements within the composition are emphasised with touches of brighter colour applied more heavily.

Many of these works have a long gestation—it takes time to assimilate and order research collected from many different sources over several years. For example, a front page from the Sun had been saved in 1994 to be used in the painting *Normandy War Graves*. The studies were started in 1998 but the painting was not completed until 2005.

The rising interest in figurative painting in the early eighties led to a reappraisal of German Expressionism and The Neue Sachlichkeit, particularly Max Beckmann, Otto Dix and George Gross. Compositionally and figuratively this had a huge influence on my work and traces of Beckmann can be seen in the cramped and claustrophobic composition

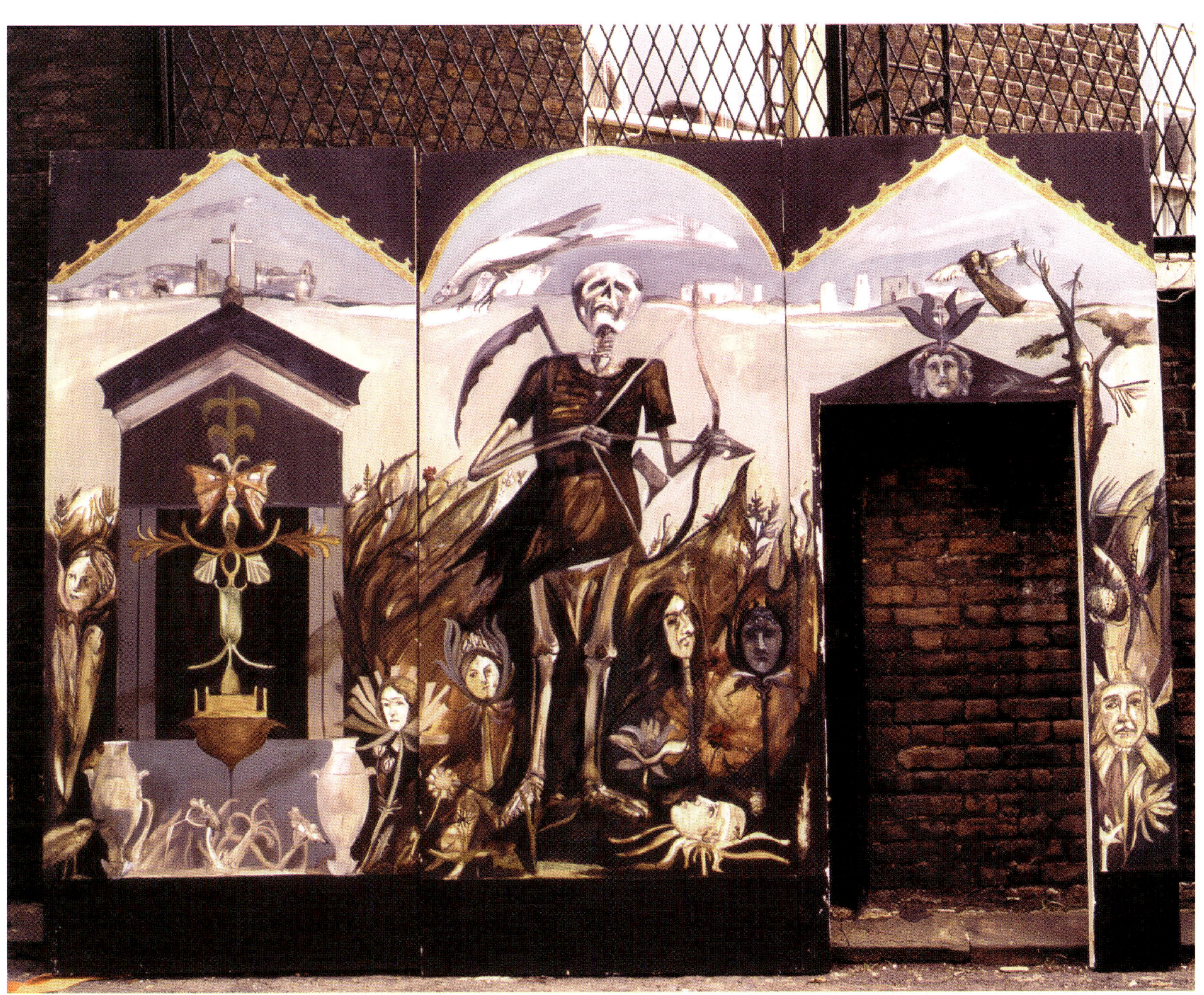

of *The Anderson Shelter*. Whilst the images are realistic, the space which they occupy is invented. In *Mothers' Sons* I use a format which I call 'shallow stage set', where the action occurs within a shallow foreground and secondary images are placed against a flattened backdrop. This can also be seen in the murals of the Villa Boscoreale in Pompeii and in the graffiti-covered wall in Ben Shahn's *Handball*. In *Shoes from Majdenek* and *Flanders Fields* the notion of the backdrop or screen is further extended with repeating images overlapping to fill the picture plane completely. Here there is no suggestion of recession or perspective but only of a mass which could extend endlessly.

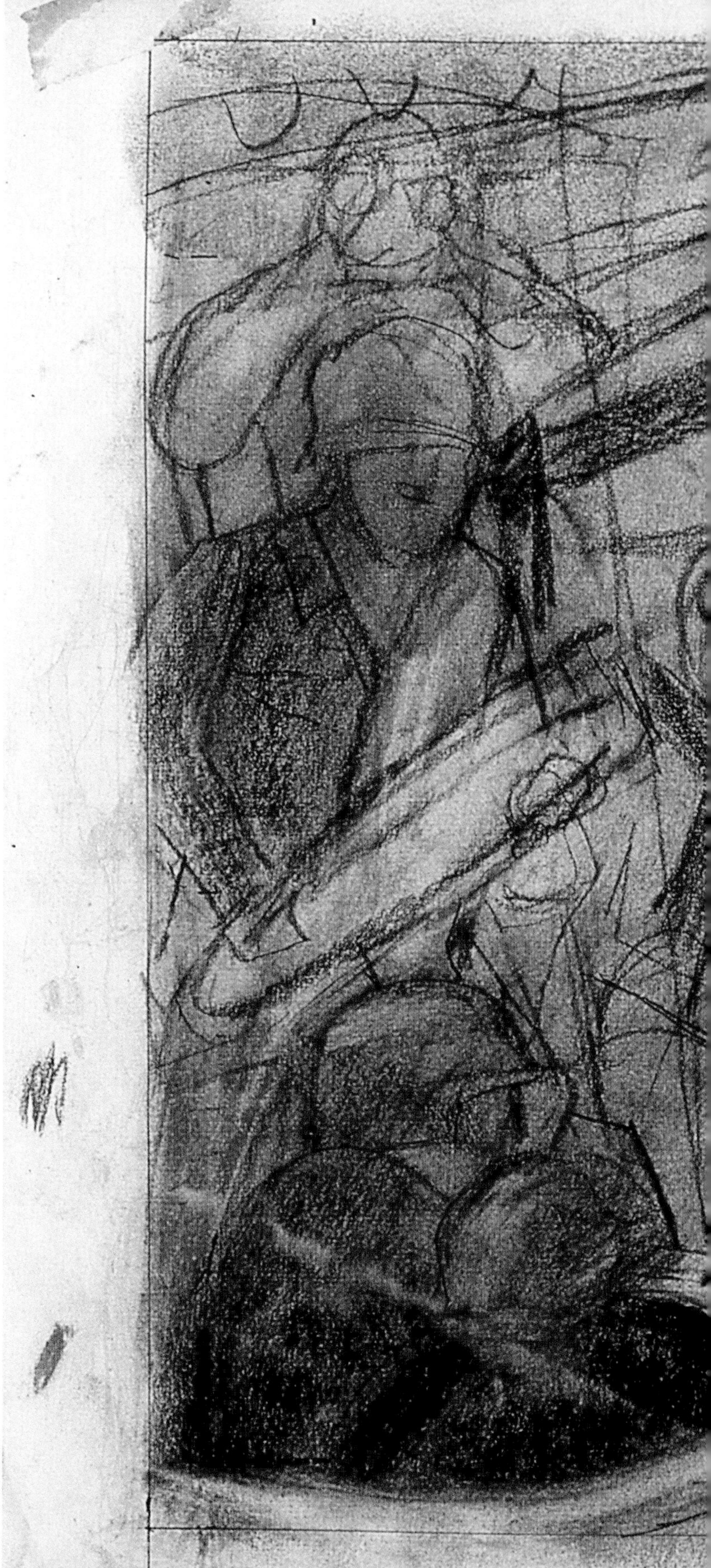

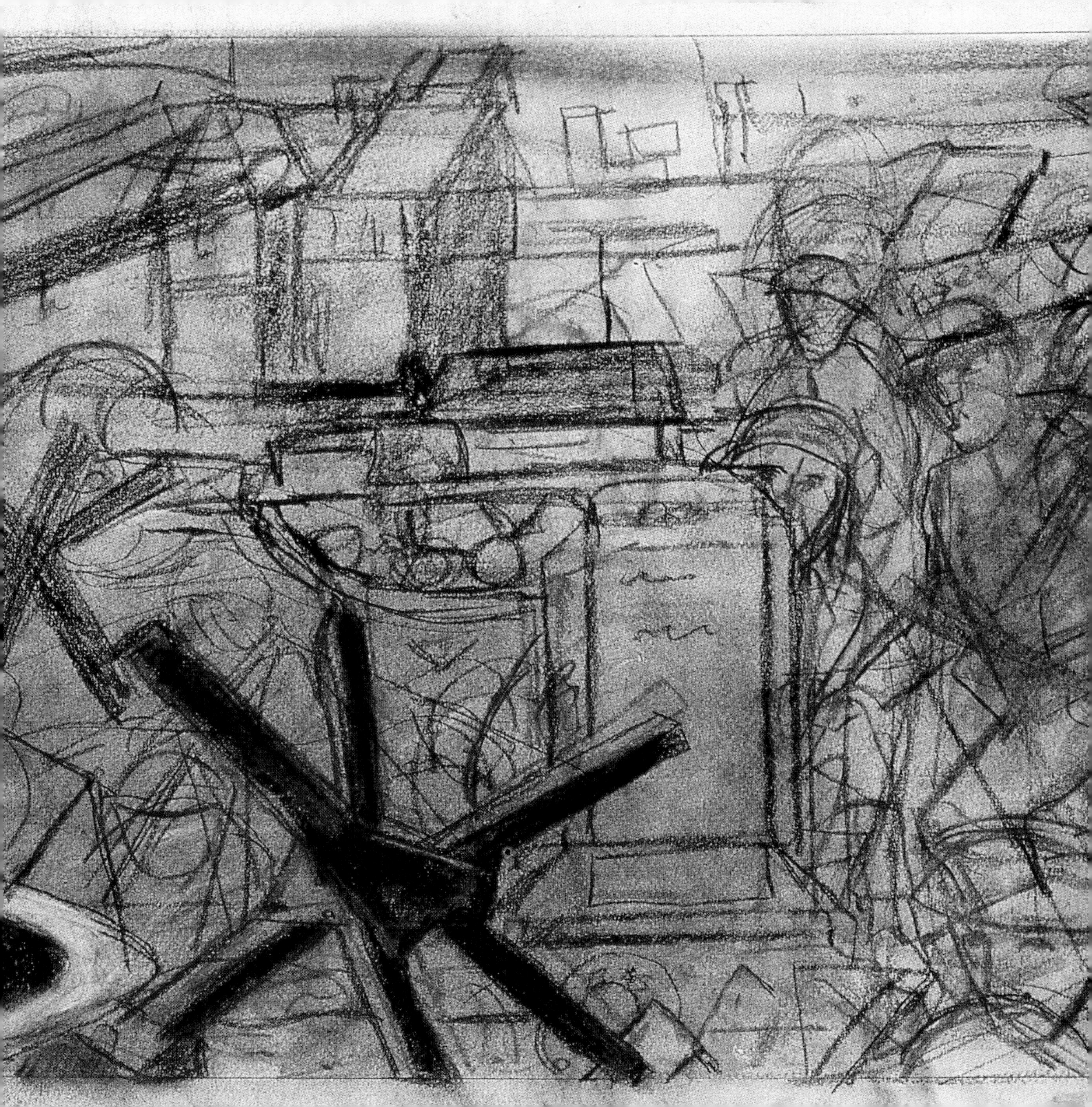

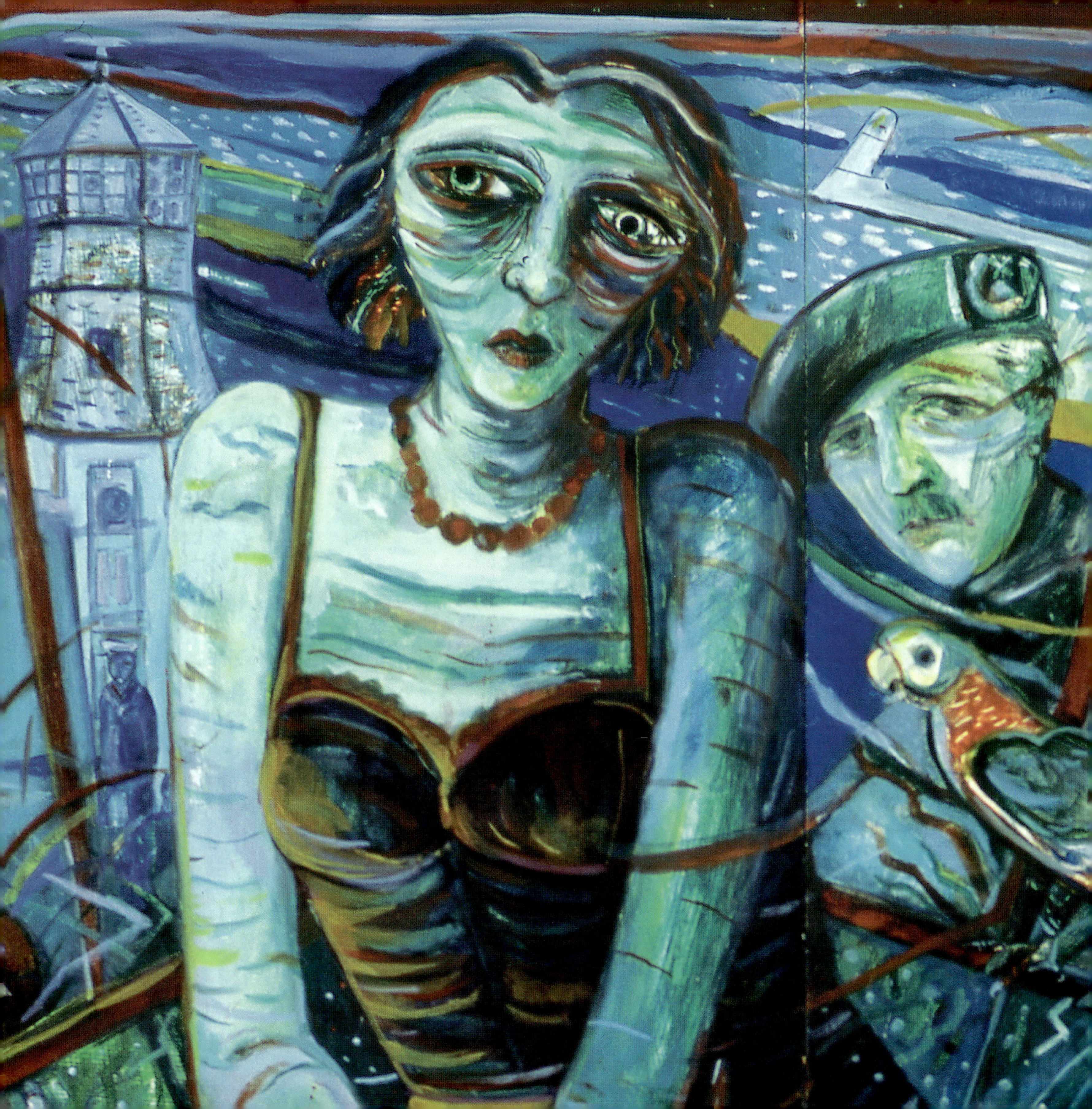

WITNESSING AND WARNING

Bill Hare

'I write what I would never dare tell anyone' – PRIMO LEVI

UNLEASH THE DOGS OF WAR! War is the most terrible curse inflicted on human history. War is the Four Men of the Apocalypse rolled into one. War spreads devastation and suffering wherever and whenever it rides. Yet, on the other hand, war, ironically, has also been the source and inspiration for some of the most memorable works of literature and art the world has ever known-from Homer's *Iliad* to Picasso's *Guernica*. In this essay I will contend that these inspiring and disturbing paintings of Joyce Cairns yet again bear witness to this continuing contradiction between the destructive force of war and the creative power of art.

By chance while writing this essay on one of Scotland's most remarkable and critically admired contemporary figurative painters, I happened to hear two news items which seemed absolutely appropriate for the thematic significance of Joyce Cairns' epic WAR TOURIST series. Firstly, it was announced that the last surviving Australian First War veteran had just died at the ripe old age of 104. Secondly, the Pentagon reported that the death toll of US troops in Iraq had just passed the symbolically significant two thousand mark. Here, yet again, we can see in stark contradistinction the same recurring concern which runs all through Joyce Cairns' work: the fundamental contrast between the war experience of one individual, hero or victim, set against the seemingly endless mass of anonymous human suffering and carnage.

While naturally the Americans wish to play down the immensity of their current war losses, the Australian government, on the other hand, is delighted to honour with a full state funeral, its last surviving combatant of a war, now safely confined to the history books. No-one of course, would oppose this appropriate gesture of public gratitude and remembrance. This is the time-honoured ritual that gives any nation a very tangible sense of its historical identity and plugs into the collective consciousness of its subjects. War by its very nature is a great mass event which seeks to involve everyone it touches in its public demonstrations of unity and solidarity, both during, and after, the time of conflict. Joyce

Cairns' paintings, however, aim to penetrate underneath this uncritical, self-decorated surface of macho military posturing and public coherence. In *War Tourist* she sets out to sympathetically explore and critically expose the more private, feminine side of our attitude to the devastating and traumatic impact of military conflict on the individual human psyche and the collective memory.

Such is the enthralling seriousness of these paintings that even someone like myself, who has little interest in military history, is still absorbed by their epic sweep of subject matter and their intense pictorial examination of human actions and responses under the most adverse and harrowing circumstances. Monumental in scale, most of these pictures of Joyce Cairns are also bursting with high emotional drama, ranging from deep pathos *(Irma)* to intense outrage *(The Drums of War)*. Clearly with such work, this dedicated and highly experienced painter has risen to the highest realms of artistic ambition and intent. In academic terms such pictures confirm that the artist has now become a contemporary history painter of immense visual rhetorical power and great moral and artistic authority, demonstrated by such 'great machines' as *The Deadly Wars*.

Amongst other things, all history painters need to demonstrate, as Joyce Cairns undoubtedly does here, that they are skilled in rendering every type of subject matter- from epic tragedy to keenly observed still life. She even manages to bring these two dimensions together in one powerful work, *After the Battle*. Furthermore, confronted with such an awesome sweep of the horrors of modern history, the viewer desperately requires a trusted presence to guide them through the seemingly endless physical and human devastation that is presented to their horrified eyes. Mercifully we are provided with the eponymous *War Tourist* who, like some ancient female deity from classical art, acts as our sympathetic medium, reflecting and transmitting our various responses to the heroic actions and deep suffering to be found in these images.

Clearly the artist is fully aware that much of what she presents in her painting is for many people extremely harrowing and profoundly disturbing. This, however, is not shock for shock's sake, as in much contemporary art. As a dedicated history painter she is required to confront the dominant historical forces of her time and convey them truthfully to her contemporaries. On the other hand, also being a modern female artist, her attitude and approach will be radically different from that of the male history painters of the past. Then, history painting was highly-esteemed because it was expected to express, in the most learned and exemplary pictorial forms, a universal understanding and celebration of human heroic and tragic actions. But with the emergence of modern ideological and technological warfare, and its awesome capacity to annihilate millions of combatants and civilians alike, the previously held Enlightenment faith in the power of human reason to understand the ways of man and historical progress was severely challenged—as was the authority of conventional academic history painting. Working now as a contemporary history painter, Joyce Cairns here re-examines and reassesses the new role and purpose of this type of painting under very different conditions from the past. Instead of vainly clinging to its earlier, and now redundant, mission of intellectually and religiously instructing its public in socially approved, ethical conduct; our artist operates, not through received wisdom and conventional instruction, but with highly expressive emotional impact and passionate empathic reaction. These history paintings of Joyce Cairns are not public pronouncements, but open discourses on the moral conditions of our age, where tragically war seems to still be endemic.

In all these works there is a distinctive female response to war, where the more personal and private dimensions operate at a different level from that of the official chronological history of reasonable cause and effect. Here we are more likely to be dealing with memory and myth as the motivating and guiding forces on human actions. Once the reassuring façade of reason and order is smashed, the artist courageously dives into the vortex of the ever-shifting, constantly-changing, realm of the human imagination. As with Picasso's *Guernica* for example, nothing is securely fixed, neither in time nor space. In such a pictorial world of fluctuating imagery, as instanced in *They Said the War was Partly to Blame* traumatic personal recollections of childhood domestic incidents merge and overlap with imagined scenes from her father's war experiences—whether in the blazing sunlit deserts of North Africa *(Longstop Hill)*, or the mine-covered beaches of Normandy *(Sword Beach)*, or the deadly silent wasteland of Holocaust Central Europe (*Polish Journey*). And all the time this real and imagined fragmented imagery from the war-torn world, both past and present, comes back to haunt and inspire the artist in the mission hall studio of her beloved Footdee village at the mouth of Aberdeen harbour. For even here war invades the lives of this small fishing community, as seen in *Messerschmitt over Footdee.*

Joyce Cairns' multilayered images reveal that, whether we like it or not, we are all touched and involved in some way by the destructive forces of human history. Mephistopheles' chilling observation to Faust that hell is here and we are all in it, seems to be abundantly confirmed today by the global village of mass media communication which is the very stuff of our nightmare electronic age. Now, if we wish we can watch people in previously inaccessible parts of the world being blown to bloody bits while we eat our *TV Dinners*. Thus in Joyce Cairns' fractured and multifaceted images the artist's array of highly personal memorabilia is constantly linking, through association and the power of memory, with the relentless forces of history outside the sanctuary of her domestic environment. Joyce Cairns' grand history painting and humble still life jostle and merge with each other. The macrocosm and microcosm overlap, creating a continuous interconnection which binds us all with the on-going historical development—through past, present and future.

This almost vertiginous sensation of whirling disequilibrium which gives such powerful vitality to many of Joyce Cairns' pictorial compositions is very much epitomised by the motif of the carousel which appears in two of her works—*The Deadly Wars* and *Irma*. This sensation of concentric spiralling motion, where the centre is barely holding all the disparate parts together, powerfully conveys the schizophrenic experience of a fragmenting reality seen from both the inner and outer worlds. But yet another, even more frightening, madness is also portrayed in these paintings. In marked contrast, both in form and mood, are the works dealing directly with that ultimate modern warfare horror—the Holocaust.

In *Auschwitz Memorial* the whole image is framed within a rigid grid to convey what Primo Levi astutely describes as the 'geometric madness' of the Nazi's Final Solution Programme of ethnic cleansing, or to put it more bluntly, annihilation. With this pictorial paranoia we are starkly confronted with the 'pitiless process of natural selection', where scientific categorisation is taken to its final insane conclusion- millions of people reduced to mere *Haftlings*, with just numbers for names. Into this totally alien world of 'primordial mechanism' the artist has valiantly attempted to bring back that most humane of artistic expression-portraiture. Portraiture, from the Latin word *protrahere*, meaning to single out from the mass, is the very antithesis of what was perpetrated on those helpless victims who were turned into a faceless mass of sub-humanity by their victimisers. In a compassionate attempt to rectify this monstrous affront to basic human respect, the artist has valiantly attempted, through the life-affirming spirit of painting itself, to resist this deadly system of total depersonalisation by giving back to the photographic images of these nameless ones their place in human history. By her painstaking dedication to her art and her subjects, the artist sympathetically strives to restore their stolen right to individual dignity and common humanity.

This total commitment to her seemingly impossible self-appointed task is most borne out by the gigantic still life painting, *Shoes from Madjanek*. Under adverse conditions (working with a magnifying glass to see poor definition photographs that she took in the huts at the camp filled to overflowing with rotting shoes), the artist has unflinchingly confronted the stark logic and pitiless madness of the Nazis ideal of the fulfilment of its vision of the Hegelian historical process. As Joyce Cairns' uncompromising picture shows, this perverted vision of Nazi historicism ends in a mountain of silent shoes, stolen from their helpless owners on their last, barefoot walk to the gas chamber, in order that these pathetic human artefacts might be re- utilised for the further glory of the Third Reich. Here for countless victimised people the process of modern history came to a grinding halt—but the artist defiantly refuses to allow their killers to have the final say.

The contrast in treatment and mood between these concentration camp images and Joyce Cairns' other war pictures, such as the lovingly rendered paintings of her father's highland regiment uniform *(Father's Memorabilia)* could not be more striking. Furthermore, in another very different work, *Sword Beach,* the artist fully demonstrates her unique pictorial narrative skills in conveying through a range of disparate means, her imagined impression of what her father might have experienced in the bloody mayhem of the D–Day Normandy landings. Thus, while such paintings are redolent with explosive action and varied incident, the subjects (whether human or not) in the concentration camp pictures are, by contrast, all equally treated with the same uniformity of attention which verges on the minimalistic. Within these Holocaust images nothing is overtly stressed and so the grotesque nature of the historical reality just behind the surface appearance is infinitely more powerfully conveyed by the matter-of-fact technique employed by the artist. Where we might have expected something 'more apocalyptic everything is as silent as an aquarium'. Thus with dedicated commitment and compassion Joyce Cairns, against all the odds *and* her natural inclinations as an intuitive narrative painter, has managed to express and convey the essential moribund nature of the concentration camps, where all human personality and emotion and vitality is drained and reduced to a deathly zero.

WAR TOURIST confirms that those long years of hard work and determined effort, where artistic skills have been honed to precision and the committed search for authentic subject matter has been relentless pursued, has now come together to produce some of the most powerful and moving paintings ever created by a Scottish artist. The range of themes and approaches developed in these works is vastly varied: from the celebration of the human sprit under the most catastrophic conditions through to the unflinching depiction of acts of monstrous barbarity. Yet, at the same time, all this is expressed and conveyed with a deeply personal and sincerely committed seriousness and compassion. In these very challenging works the artist shows us that even in the face of the most incomprehensible and inexplicable acts of man's inhumanity to man, the empathic power of the human spirit and the sympathetic imagination can survive, and even triumph, over all the evils that are carried out in the name of war. With the constant reassuring female presence of the WAR TOURIST to sustain and guide us through the horrors of recent and current human affairs, we, as individuals and as a society of kindred spirits, might still be able to survive in a war-torn world that even now has to learn the lessons of history. In the end it will only be when we are both able to follow the way of the WAR TOURIST, and also readily heed the voice of the survivor (that it is always preferable 'to witness than to judge') that we may hopefully look forward to a war-free future.

Ironically, by facing up to what we might all wish to avoid seeing, it is this strange disturbing beauty of Joyce Cairns' war-torn paintings that truly bears witness to this cherished ideal.

All quotations come from *If this is a man* by Primo Levi, first published in 1958.

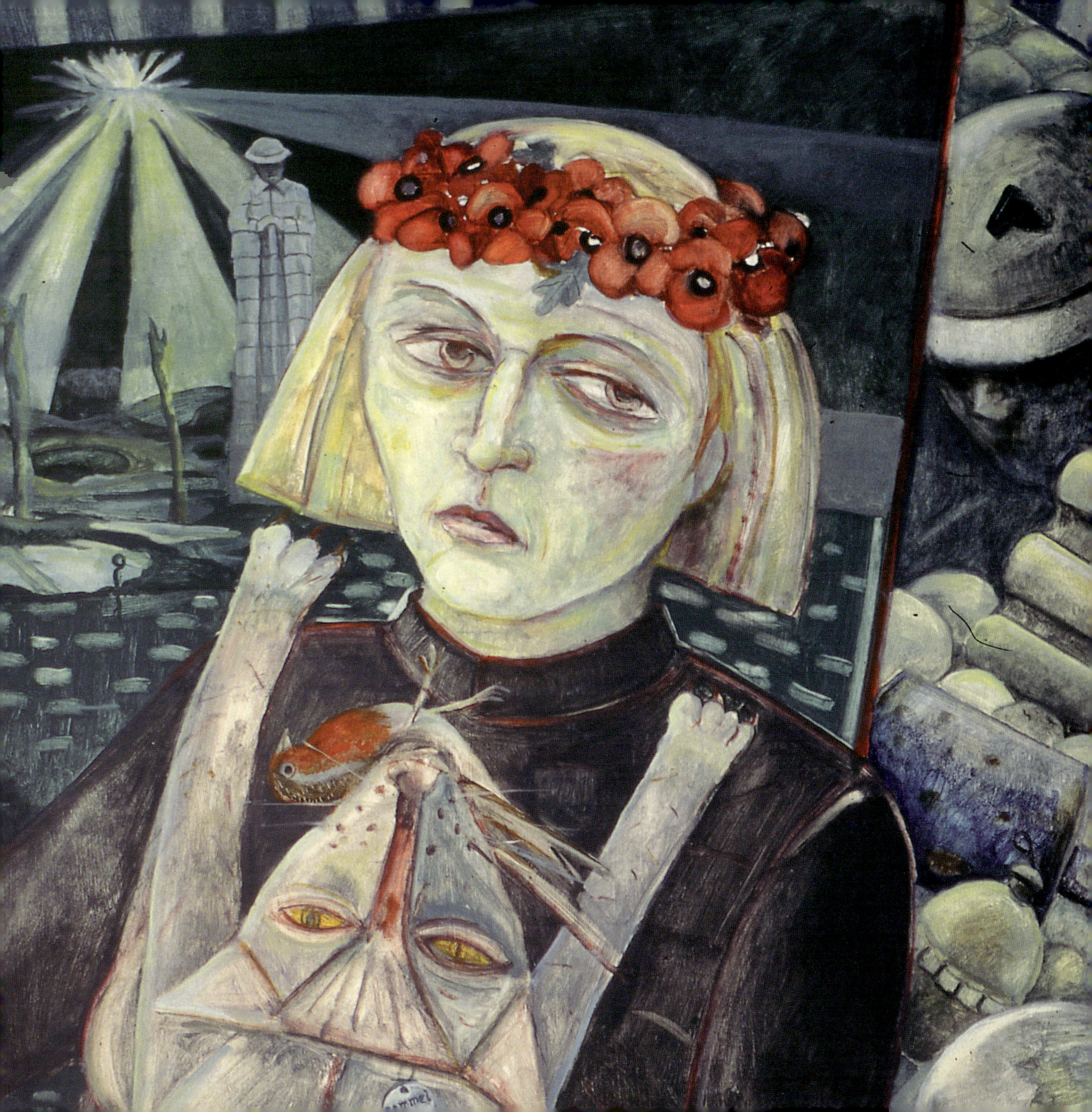

Opposite, left

PLATE TWO

Father's Memorabilia, Tunisia, 1995
Oil on panel, 183 × 122 cm

Opposite, right

PLATE THREE

Father's Memorabilia, North West Europe, 1995
Oil on panel, 183 × 122 cm

My elder brother is the keeper of the family archive and in 1995 he showed me a battered suitcase containing my father's wartime memorabilia—medals, uniforms, testimonials, photographs and postcards. I was very excited to have them with me in Aberdeen where they became my inspiration and a key resource. A pair of German binoculars and the sword presented to my father by a surrendering German Officer are with other family members. My first task was to group these chronologically and formally compose them as preparation for a pair of paintings. This was a new departure, as still life on its own has never had much appeal but I found these objects, so emotionally charged with the presence of their wearer and his part in history, that an actual figurative input was unnecessary.

When I started to paint the kilt I realised that it seemed very small—then, remembering that it had been cut down to fit me, enlarged it again in the painting.

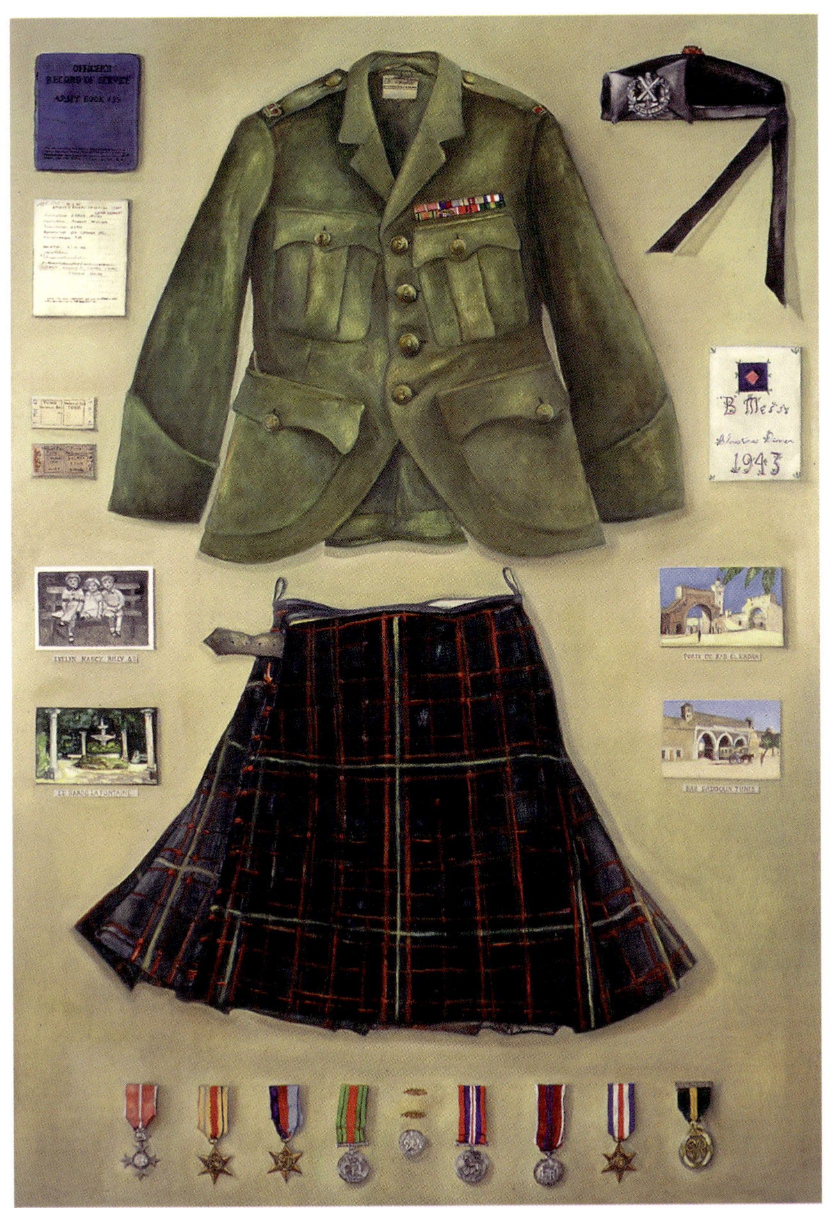

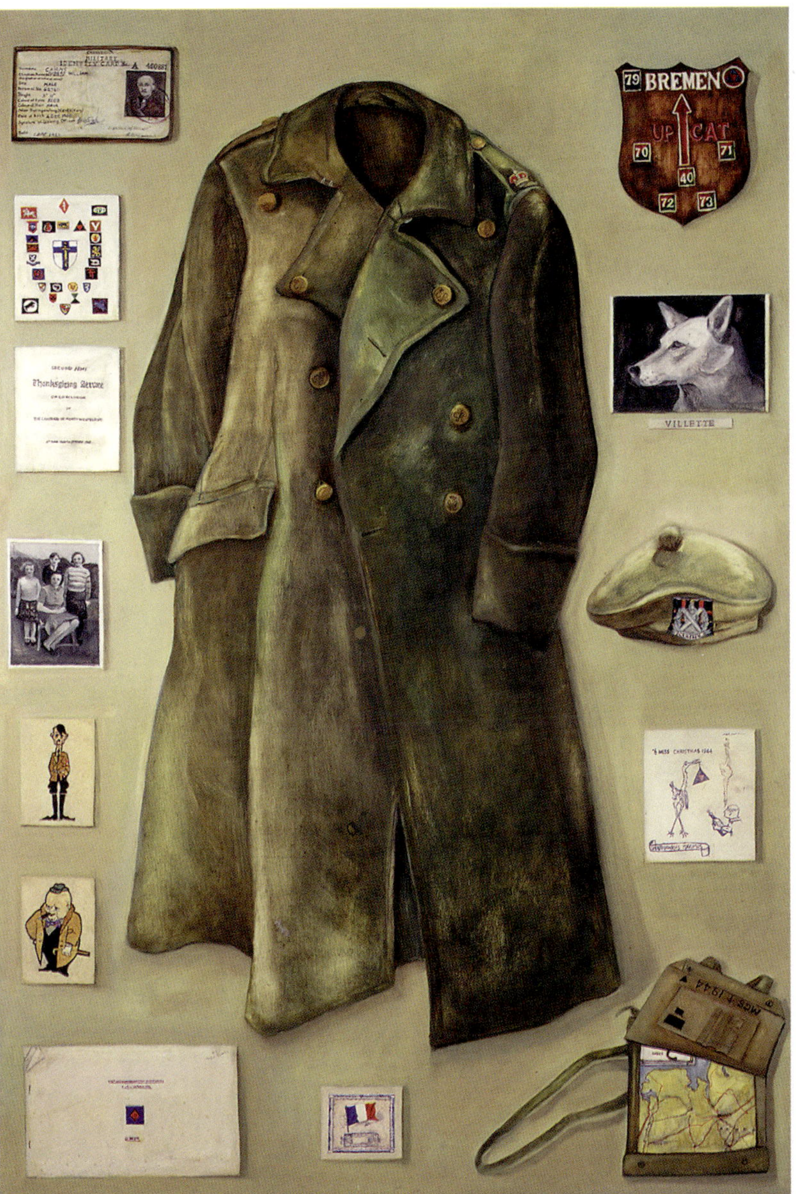
BREMEN
UP CAT
VILLETTE

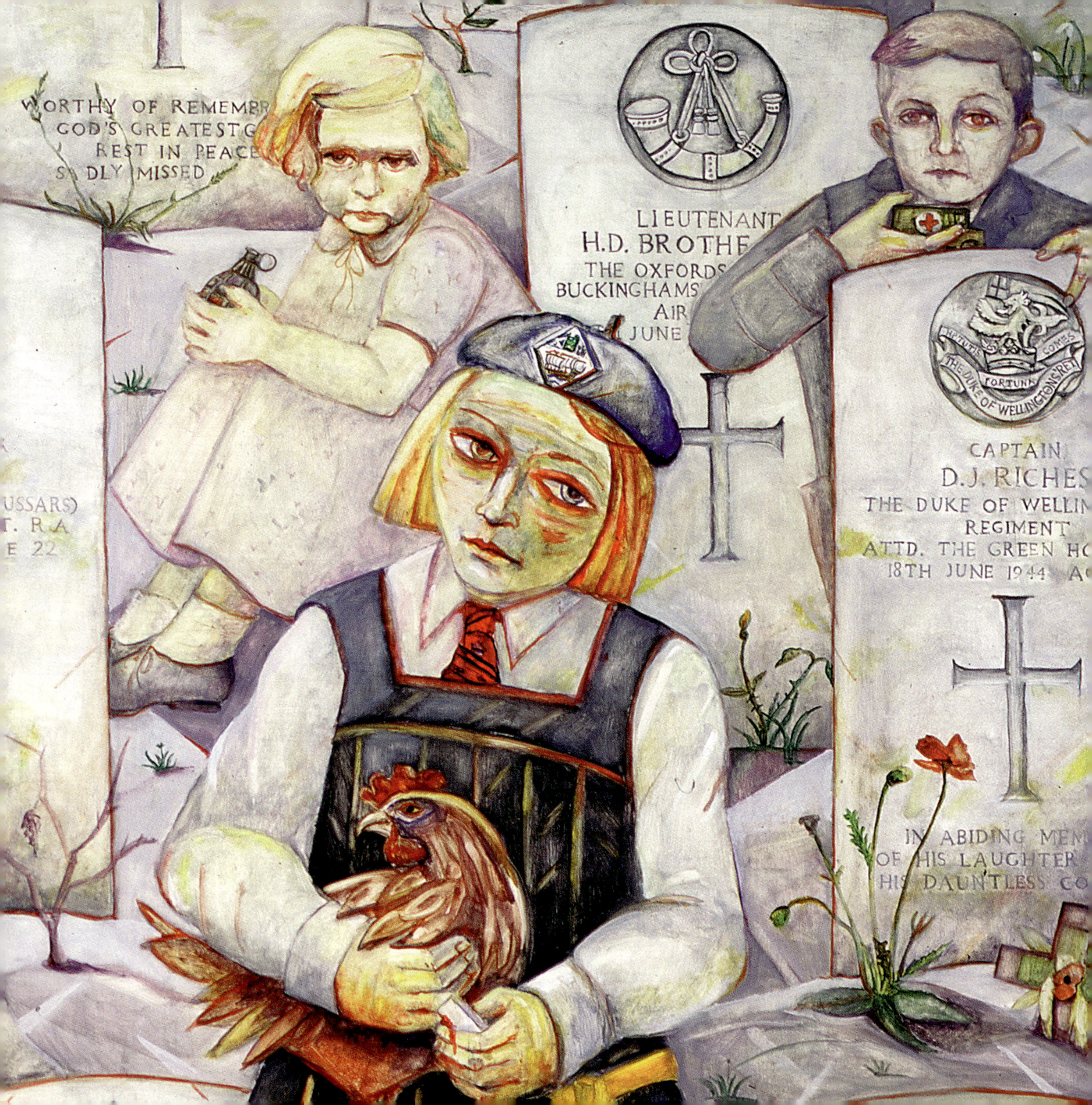

WORTHY OF REMEMBR
GOD'S GREATEST G
REST IN PEACE
SADLY MISSED
LIEUTENANT
H.D. BROTHE
THE OXFORDS
BUCKINGHAMS
AIR
JUNE
USSARS)
T. R.A
E 22
FORTUNA
THE DUKE OF WELLINGTONS REGT
CAPTAIN
D.J. RICHES
THE DUKE OF WELLIN
REGIMENT
ATTD. THE GREEN HO
18TH JUNE 1944 A
IN ABIDING MEM
OF HIS LAUGHTER
HIS DAUNTLESS CO

MAJOR ROBERT CAIRNS, HIS WAR

Stuart Allan

JOYCE CAIRNS travelled to the scenes of her father's war armed only with clues. Like many of those with personal memories of warfare, Major Robert Cairns did not speak casually of his experiences and left no memoir or diary that could inform an itinerary. But that which he did leave was nevertheless sufficient to arouse and inform a daughter's need to affirm what her father had done, to follow some of the paths he took during the Second World War in those years of heightened experience that conveyed him and the men of his generation away from the familiar world of home, family and work. The things he did leave behind, tangible *things*, artefacts, appear and reappear in Joyce's paintings. Insignia and uniform, postcards and photographs: these items are the stock in trade for those of us who record and interpret the history of warfare through collections of objects. Such are the things that are commonly kept by those who have experienced military service as relics of a period in their lives which had a lasting effect upon them. Moved to hold on to these things, they might rarely, perhaps never, look them out, but remain reluctant to dispose of them and so break the connection to times when action, danger and a sense of shared purpose brought a quickening to their lives. It is often their children, not they themselves, who bring these things to the attention of museums, after the original owner has died, feeling they have inherited something they have no business to discard. Passing them to a public collection, they hope not only to enhance the historical record but seek also to preserve and honour the person and the events he lived through, and to discharge their responsibility to both.

Joyce Cairns inherited a desk-full of mementoes of this kind. They set her off on her travels and gave her an eye for the material culture of warfare relating to other times and places. Not leaving it to curators and historians to make what use of them they would, Joyce has arranged them into her own travelogue. In these paintings they surround her in a narrative that is first of all about herself and her family, about her connection to what her father did before she was born. The Second World War affected families profoundly, but, particularly in those families where men were sent on active service overseas, the experience was not a shared one. The men were away from home for long periods; their experiences were new and unfamiliar—not just in the extremes of combat but in travel and in attuning to a different, communal way of life in which their families did not figure. They in turn were removed from the privations their families faced at home, detached from the domestic and emotional consequences of their own absence. It is not to suggest that all men enjoyed every aspect of active military service to acknowledge that undoubtedly some actively did. However much they might have missed home and family, military life suited some. Even in boredom, frustration and danger, and in longing for its end, the experience of warfare shared with comrades, a surrogate family, could make the war years the most memorable and meaningful times of their lives. Their families might sense this feeling of belonging, and their own distance from it.

On the outbreak of war in 1939 Robert Cairns was, at 32, older than many men called up for war service. As headmaster at Cawdor School, Nairn, he had professional responsibilities. He had been married for nearly nine years and had three children. He had also been prepared for the possibility and practice of war. He was, properly, Captain R.W. Cairns, his attraction and commitment to the military life demonstrated in five years of part-time service as a Territorial Army officer. Commissioned into a Territorial battalion of his local regiment the Queen's Own Cameron Highlanders in 1934, the TA diet of weekend training and annual camps meant Captain Cairns was one of those trained volunteer soldiers deemed ready for immediate mobilisation and deployment in 1939 while the calling-up and training of the conscripted civilian population was just getting underway. His peacetime military know-how as a Motor Transport Officer meant however that he was not to accompany his Cameron battalion on active service as it proceeded south in 1940 and on across the Channel to the defence of France. Instead, with an appointment as Transport Officer of 26th Infantry Brigade, his experience was put towards the raising and training of a new Territorial Army formation in northern Scotland, the 9th (Highland) Division. Starting with little by way of vehicles to work with, his task was to realise the mobility of mobile infantry, applying principles of road discipline on long and complex motor-transport moves. But before much progress with equipping or training could be made, Captain Cairns met with a mishap that shaped the course of his war; a vehicle accident left him with a damaged back and unfit for further infantry service.

Captain Cairns' recovery coincided with a pressing demand for capable personnel from a corps of the British army that, like many others, was expanding rapidly to meet the requirements of a major war. The Corps of Military Police may have lacked something of the tradition and glamour of a highland infantry regiment—and Captain Cairns was to be resolute in remaining a Cameron Highlander for the duration—but to the Military Police, or 'Provost', an increasingly vital function had fallen, one to which an infantry officer accustomed to organising transport could readily contribute. The calamitous Allied defeat in the battle of France in the early summer of 1940 (which saw Captain Cairns' old battalion of the Cameron Highlanders marched into four years of captivity) revealed serious deficiencies in the organisation and planning of military operations. One lesson was that the rapid movement of fighting formations and supplies, towards and away from the enemy, through a basic and complex road network frequently shared with civilian refugees, required a highly efficient system for regulating military traffic. This capability had already been developed by the Corps of Military Police during the First World War, an addition to its traditional function of preventing and investigating military crime. Now, as Britain faced the real possibility of German invasion in 1940, the question of military traffic control had to be applied with some urgency to the possible need to supply and re-enforce a fighting front upon the British mainland itself. By June 1941, when Captain Cairns was seconded to the Corps of Military Police, that most desperate phase of Britain's European war had passed and the Home Forces were turning their efforts towards preparing instead for future offensive operations. These, it was already realised, would at some stage necessarily involve assault landings on enemy-held coastline by a force capable of securing and holding a beachhead onto which men and supplies could be poured. The assembly of such an assault force would itself require a rigorous system of planning and control for traffic routes. That achieved, if successful assault landings were to develop into a meaningful offensive that could penetrate deep into enemy territory, then the system of signing and controlling operational traffic routes to and from the frontline, to transit, assembly and supply areas had to be prepared, resourced and carried out meticulously. Blocked roads or roads damaged by unnecessary overuse could mean opportunities missed, could ultimately mean failure. The responsibilities of the Military Policeman in a war of movement were to be heavy; they could also put him close to the front line of offensive operations.

After briefly commanding a Provost Company of Military Policemen, Captain Cairns was appointed Deputy Assistant Provost Marshal of 61st Infantry Division and was soon promoted to Assistant Provost Marshal of the same formation with the temporary (wartime) rank of Major. A divisional 'APM' was responsible for liaising with headquarters staff in planning and enforcing workable traffic

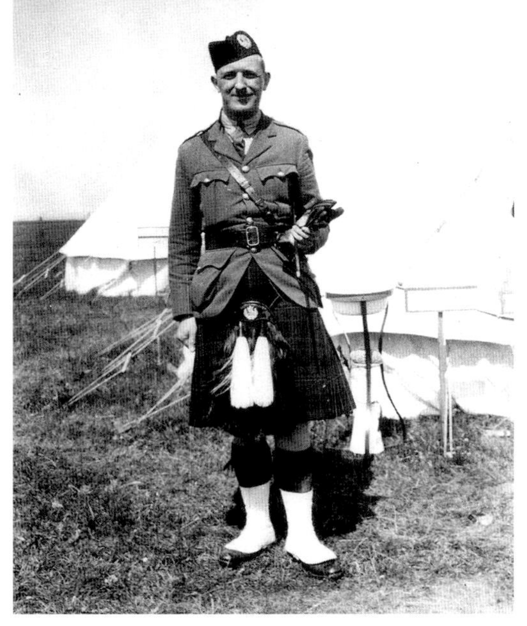

Lieutenant R.W. Cairns, 4th Battalion Queen's Own Cameron Highlanders, c1937.

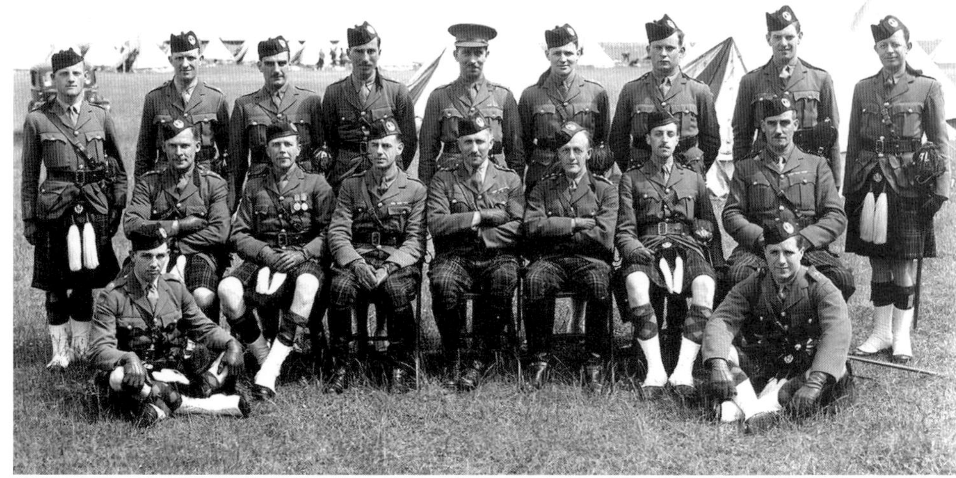

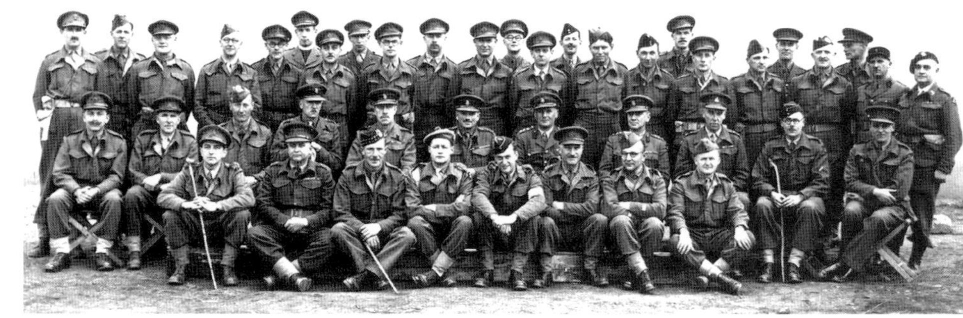

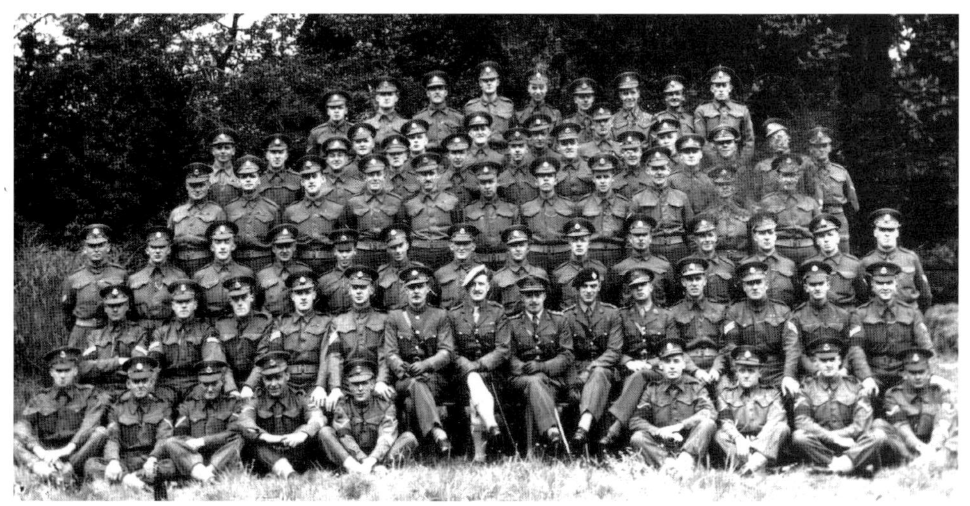

RIGHT HAND COLUMN, TOP TO BOTTOM

Officers of 4th (Territorial) Battalion, Queen's Own Cameron Highlanders at Tain camp, 1935. 2nd Lieutenant R.W. Cairns stands in the rear row, second from left.

5 Corps headquarters staff, February 25th 1943. Corps Commander Lieutenant-General C.W. Allfrey is seated at centre of the second row, Major Cairns is standing third from right.

Major R.W. Cairns MBE, seated at centre of front row, with 61st Division Provost personnel, south-east England, June 1st 1944.

RIGHT HAND COLUMN, TOP TO BOTTOM

Major R.W. Cairns MBE checks traffic plans with 3rd Division Provost personnel, north-west Europe, c1944.

Captain Cairns with a fellow officer and men of 51st (Highland) Division, c1939.

'A soldier and his friend',
Major R.W. Cairns MBE with 'Villette',
northwest Europe, c1944.

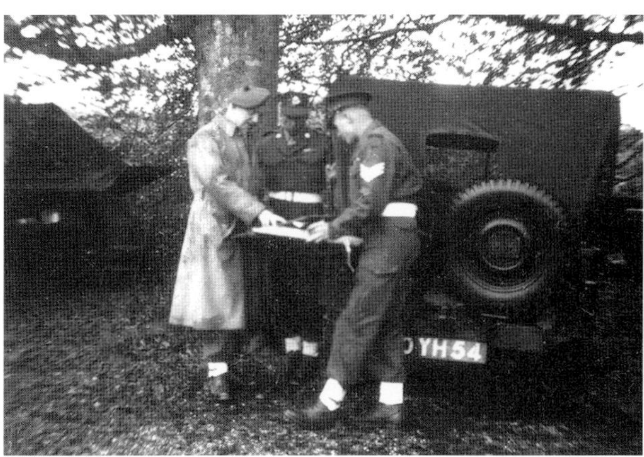

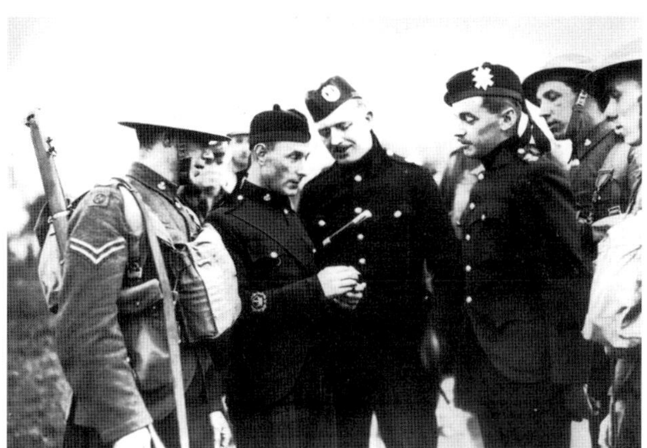

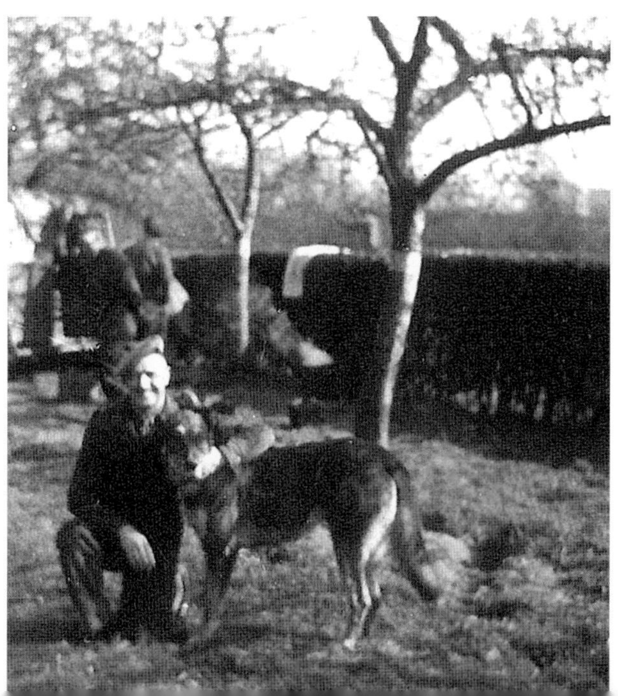

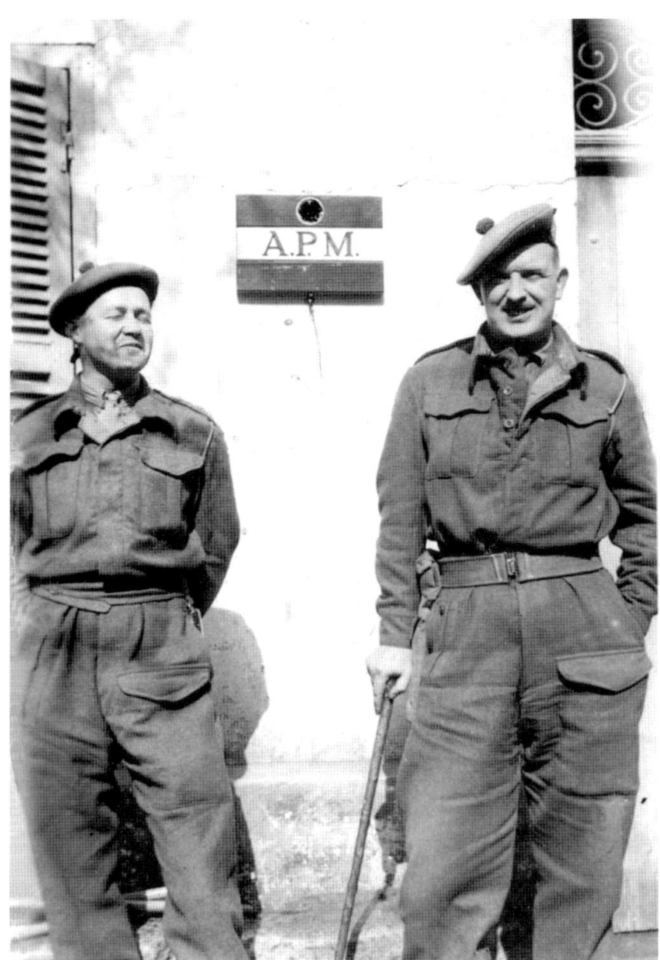

Major R.W. Cairns, Assistant Provost Marshal 5 Corps, with a fellow officer outside his headquarters office, Tunisia, March 21st 1943.

control plans for his division. The main fighting tool of an army, a division comprised a force of infantry with contingents of artillery, engineer, transport and supply and medical services that could total over fifteen thousand men, could run over half as many vehicles, and which might be supplied and maintained in action by near twice as many men again in support. If a division was to fight, it had to be able to move—in advance or retreat—and move in harmony with the formations around it; it was the job of the Assistant Provost Marshal and his divisional Military Police to ensure that it did.

61st Infantry Division was a second-line formation; stationed in Northern Ireland until 1943 to guard against any German incursion into Eire, it remained in the UK throughout the war. But its diet of regular training exercises and manoeuvres created a pool of trained staff available to be called upon for operational service in other formations. So it was that Major Cairns was despatched at the end of 1942 to Allied Force Headquarters North Africa at Algiers. The desert war had raged back and forth across huge expanses of territory for some two years, but, at the turn of 1942, it was approaching its endgame. Following the great victory at El Alamein, General Montgomery's 8th Army had advanced west from Egypt, pushing German and Italian forces back through Libya. In November, successful Allied amphibious landings in French Morocco and Algeria had seen the British 1st Army overcome resistance from Vichy French forces and advance east to confront the German forces that had been poured into Tunisia. It was while both sides were consolidating their positions and preparing for the battle for northeast Tunisia that Major Cairns arrived in North Africa. From Allied Forces Headquarters he was soon despatched to be Assistant Provost Marshal of 5 Corps, with responsibility for the Military Police element of this the northernmost tactical grouping of 1st Army. This was still essentially a headquarters job, but one on operational service nonetheless and Major Cairns' appointment was occasioned by the death of his predecessor as APM 5 Corps, mortally wounded when his vehicle was shot up by German aircraft. The 5 Corps administrative area stretched back west from the Tunisia front-line towards northern Algeria. Cairn's Military Police had to contend with the paucity and poor quality of roads in the region supplying the build-up into Tunisia, and he was still to be much concerned with the maintenance of order and discipline in Algerian towns such as Constantine where the lure of local wine and women was getting the better of off-duty soldiers.

The lull in fighting ended rather sooner than the Allies had anticipated. In February 1943 German armoured thrusts suddenly made headway into American positions around the Kasserine Pass and, as 5 Corps sent reinforcements south to their Allies' aid, the 5 Corps front itself came under attack. For Major Cairns, the danger was prefaced with an air attack which damaged his office at Souk el Arba. With the defenders thinly strewn over dispersed positions, the enemy armoured assault in the north, codenamed 'Ochsenkopf' (Bull's Head), quickly became serious for 5 Corps. In three weeks of confused fighting, rapid withdrawals and counter-attacks had to be mounted and maintained. Engineers and military police working to keep the roads open were called upon, on occasion, to take post as infantry and while the attacks were resisted and rebuffed at the front, further to the west the APM 5 Corps co-ordinated traffic moves at advance Corps headquarters in co-operation with his counterparts at divisional level.

The ultimate failure of 'Operation Ochsenkopf' left the German army in northern Tunisia a spent force and it was the Allies' turn to attack. 1st Army finally launched its main assault towards Tunis and Bizerta in late April 1943, 5 Corps attacking along the banks of the Medjerda River and the last Axis enclave in North Africa was quickly and firmly crushed between the advances of 1st and 8th Armies. For the Corps of Military Police, the demands of keeping the necessary transport moving were compounded by the new problem of removing and containing the flow of enemy prisoners-of-war moving in number in the opposite direction. The fall of Tunis on 7th May completed the hard-fought and costly Allied victory. Among the souvenirs of service kept by Major Cairns, one that now features in his daughter's paintings, is a railway ticket bought on that day for a journey from 5 Corps headquarters at Medjez-el-Bab to Tunis.

The closing of the campaign in North Africa gave Major Cairns a part in one agreeable task, organising the victory parade held in Tunis of 20th May. And after the representatives of British, US and French forces had completed their march in triumph past Generals Eisenhower, Alexander and Giraud on the saluting-base, he returned to the prosaic practicalities of maintaining order in the newly occupied territories while the forces in the region reorganised and looked towards the invasion of Sicily. By this time he was Major R.W. Cairns MBE, his personal contribution to the 5 Corps campaign in North Africa and the orderly control of the city of Tunis rewarded with Membership of the Order of the British Empire (Military Division). His MBE recommendation*, authorised by Lieutenant-General C.W. Allfrey commanding 5 Corps, made particular reference too of the offensive operations around Medjez el Bab in late April and early May.

Unlike many men of 1st and 8th Armies in

* Much depended on the speed with which the great mass of transport, both fighting and administrative, could be got across the Mejarda and the very limited number of roads and tracks east of Medjez, and the success with which this was achieved was largely due to Major Cairns.

Lieutenant-General C.W. Allfrey

North Africa, Major Cairns was not destined for the Italian campaign. His wife's fragile health brought about a return to the UK on compassionate grounds and by the end of 1943 he was back in position as Assistant Provost Marshal of 61st Infantry Division stationed in southeast England. When the Allied invasion force landed on the Normandy beaches on 6th June 1944, 61st Division remained on the English side of the Channel, their diet of training and guard duties largely unchanged. But as the Normandy bridgehead was reinforced and expanded, and as casualties mounted, Home Forces provided the trained drafts that were needed in France and at the end of July, Major Cairns was once again sent into a theatre of operations. With his appointment as Assistant Provost Marshal of 3rd British Infantry Division, he joined a formation battle-hardened by sustained fighting in Normandy and took on a role in immediate support of the advance more mobile than that of his 5 Corps days in North Africa. 3rd Division had landed on 'Sword' beach on D-Day, and for four weeks had held the line before prevailing in a bloody contest for the heavily fortified town of Caen. When Major Cairns joined 3rd Division at the end of July 1944, more open country in southern Normandy was within its reach but with the enemy in full retreat, its advance had to be supplied from the beaches and supported through close country with a barely adequate network of roads and country lanes. The word 'congestion' is ubiquitous in accounts of the Normandy break-out; it was for the Provost Corps to unlock it with 24-hour traffic plans, consistent signing and swift road clearance when blocks occurred.

During much of August and September 1944 3rd Division enjoyed a spell out of the front line but its next deployment was to be some 200 miles distant in the Somme region, a move requiring the efficient transport of the entire divisional apparatus, including some 120,000 gallons of fuel, across road sectors already under heavy pressure from the movement of other formations. Somewhere during his service in France, possibly at Villers-en-Vexin across the Seine, Major Cairns acquired the canine company of an injured Alsatian whom he named Villette, saw back to health and kept with him for the remainder of a campaign which was to take him through France, the Low Countries and into Germany itself. His first major operation was 'Market Garden', the celebrated but unsuccessful attempt to shorten the war by a daring, rapid push into the Netherlands, connecting up with three Airborne divisions dropped to secure strategic bridges. 3rd Division's job was to protect the right flank of the advance. 'Market Garden' failed to achieve its objectives but it took 3rd Division over the Dutch frontier and into sustained fighting in the Netherlands through the month of October. In this, Operation 'Aintree', 3rd Division liberated the towns of Overloon and Venraij in face of determined German resistance and despite sustaining heavy casualties. Downfalls of rain broke up the complicated ground of muddy fields and farm tracks, and to the man-made obstacles of extensive minefields were added traffic control problems in the bottleneck approaches to the Molen Beek river, crossed on bridges constructed by the Royal Engineers. The weather was only to worsen and the resistance to stiffen but the success of 'Aintree' brought a welcome pause in offensive operations for 3rd Division, a respite which lasted through the worst of the winter. But brought forward again for the advance to the Rhine, the Division's traffic had to be moved across the waterlogged country of the winter's thaw. That country was, at last, Germany itself. In addition to the problems of convoy transportation on mud-bound roads, of signing, lighting and policing the Division's axis of advance, Major Cairns had to reckon with a hostile population controlled through curfew and in certain operational areas, compulsory evacuation. Even the movement of livestock had to be directed so as not to interfere with the supply of the front.

3rd Division's spring of fighting in Germany concluded with one final assault. The battle for the northern city of Bremen began on 13th April 1945. During two weeks of fighting, 3rd Division slowly pushed through Bremen's outlying towns and suburbs to the west, across flooded ground fiercely contested by a desperate assembly of half-trained SS youths, 'Volkssturm' home guard, submarine and anti-aircraft crews deployed as infantry, local police and firemen. As far as operations permitted, the Divisional Military Police carried out the signing of the routes in and out of the city. The two main arteries for the operation were designated CAT and RAT. UP CAT was the forward route into the city by way of Erichshof, Brinkum and Kattensturm. Amongst Major Cairn's effects, a feature in Joyce Cairn's paintings, a plaque emblazoned UP CAT TO BREMEN and bearing 3rd Division Military Police and Royal Army Service Corps vehicle markings, is therefore decoded as a personal souvenir of the part of the Military Police in that final victory. Bremen surrendered on the 26th April. The general ceasefire sounded on 5th May. Major Cairns' services in northwest Europe were recognised with a Mention in Despatches. By November 1945 he was home.

True to the Territorial Army commitment he had followed before the war, Major Cairns' military career was to continue until 1961 as he combined his work as General Manager of the Scottish National Camps Association with part-time service as a Military Policeman.

In 1947 the Corps of Military Police received the royal recognition merited by its essential part in the campaigns of the Second World War, and it was in the renamed Royal Military Police that Robert Cairns was to serve after receiving his Territorial Army full commission as a Major. In 1949 he received the Efficiency Decoration for long service in the Territorial Army. Joyce Cairns recalls a childhood in which her father spent time away at training camps in the UK and in Germany: 'he seemed to be in uniform much of the time as I remember'. There was evidently something in the life of a soldier that appealed to him strongly. The hoard of souvenirs that he accumulated, and kept, testifies to a life in which military service was a defining factor. The mementoes of his service career were not something he would have discarded casually. In Joyce's paintings these have found a new and unusual existence.

For Joyce Cairns, war tourism was a journey into her family's past that became an adventure in itself. Even without the threatening presence of Rommel's armoured divisions, or of the endless convoys of vehicles and the barely-passable roads, her travels became memorable episodes which she recalled and preserved in photographs and souvenirs and which she now presents to us in the anecdotes and allegories of her paintings. For those of us who never experience it, for all that we might self-consciously lament and revile it, war holds a fascination. Great Britain's war against Nazi Germany seemed then and seems now morally sound, and, as our former enemies are wont to notice, we feel free to indulge our interest. As a society we are today a little more circumspect in celebrating success in war than once we were, but still we cannot leave the subject alone. Amidst the nostalgic commemorations of 50th and 60th anniversaries, on the tide of books, television and film offerings on the subject, a hint of envy manifests itself, a sense among the generations who came later that they might have missed out on something significant, a nagging doubt that, perhaps, they are the poorer for not having been so tested. This is part of the culture of warfare with an ancient heritage. And for the participants, the experience of war, however disagreeable, was and remains compelling. It is remembered not just with pride and sadness, but with real fondness. It might indeed be maintained that without its redeeming qualities, war could not happen. It is perhaps only in their stark absence, as Joyce Cairns found in her visits to the concentration camps sites of the east, that we find war truly shocking.

Archival Sources

MINISTRY OF DEFENCE

Army Personnel Centre,
Record of Service,
Officers:
Major R.W. Cairns MBE, TD

NATIONAL ARCHIVES, KEW

WO171
War diaries,
North West Europe:
3rd British Division

WO175
War diaries,
British North Africa Forces,
5 Corps General and
Administrative Headquarters

WO373
War Office and Ministry
of Defence,
Honours and Awards for
Gallant and Distinguished
Service Citations

Published Sources

Blaxland, G.,
The Plain Cook and the Great Showman. The First and Eighth Armies in North Africa,
London: William Kimber, 1977

Crozier, Major S.F.,
The History of the Corps of Royal Military Police,
Aldershot: Gale and Polden, 1951

Delaforce, P.,
Monty's Ironsides. From the Normandy Beaches to Bremen with the 3rd Division,
Stroud: Alan Sutton Publishing, 1995

Playfair, Maj-Gen I.S.O. et al,
The Mediterranean and Middle East,
Official History of the Second World War
Volume iv,
London: HMSO, 1966

79th News,
The Journal of the Queen's Own Cameron Highlanders

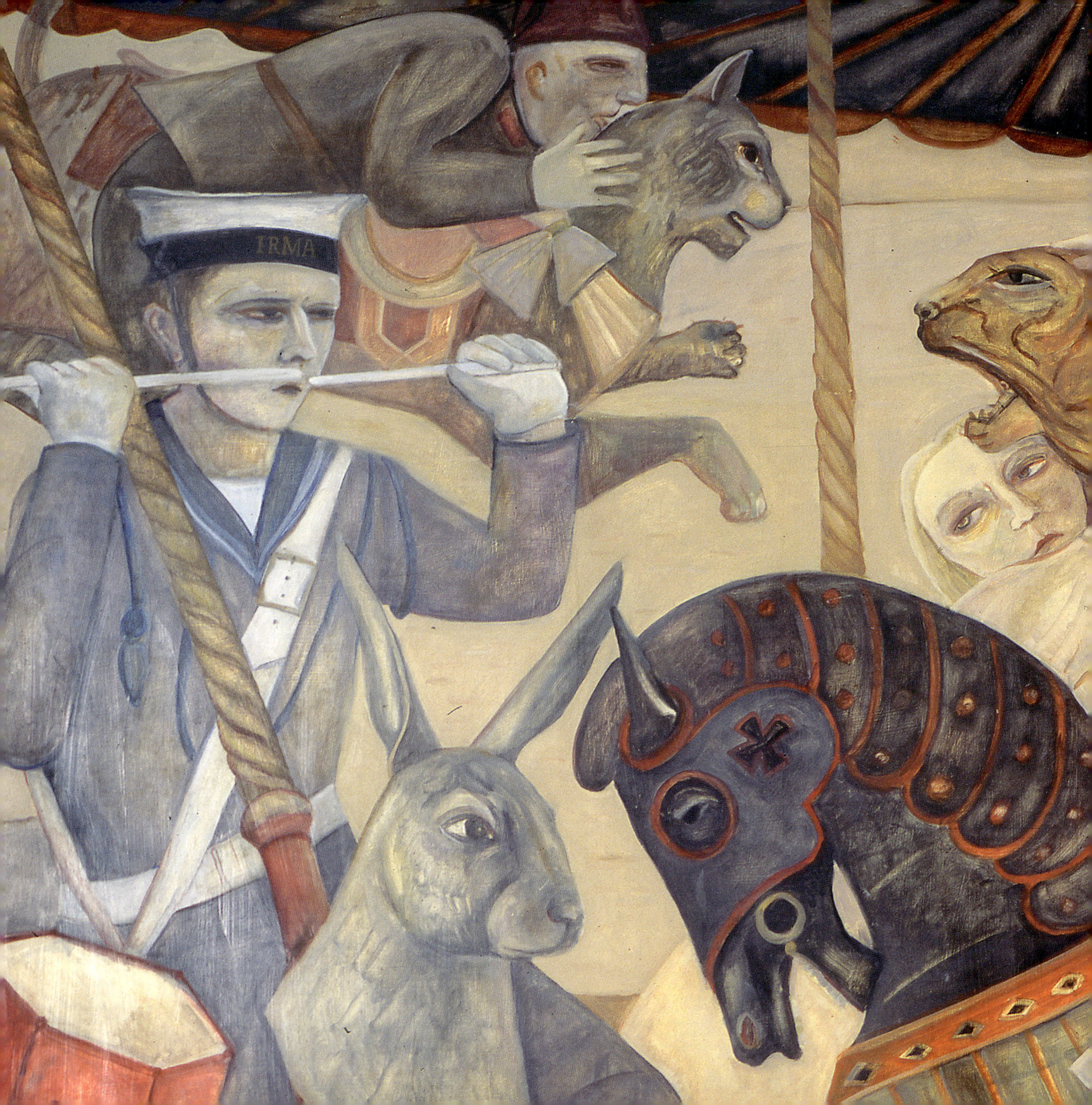

WAR TOURIST

Alexander Moffat

War as a subject has always been present in European art, persisting throughout history in ever varying forms. For many centuries paintings of war showed only victorious battles and heroic leaders. In such cases the subject was essentially the same: victory in war under the leadership of an all-powerful ruler who was usually the patron of the work. There were of course notable exceptions to this orthodoxy. Pieter Brueghel the Elder's *Slaughter of the Innocents in Bethlehem*, painted around 1564, communicates an aspect of war with which we are all too familiar at the beginning of the 21st century. Likewise, Velázquez in his *The Surrender of Breda*, painted in 1634–35, reflects an attitude and ideology which sets him apart from the tradition of victorious battle pictures referred to above. With Velázquez there are no triumphant generals or humiliated armies. But it is only in the last two hundred years, in the period since the French Revolution, or putting it another way, from the time of Goya, that artists have been free to reveal the ignominy and ruthlessness of war.

The history of the 20th century is in large part a record of war, violence and genocide. This is reflected in the works of art produced by the experience of war. The harsh and distorted images of Max Beckmann and Otto Dix, based upon their experiences at the front during World War I, confront us with the brutal reality of trench warfare. At the same time Paul Nash showed war as a destroyer of landscape and machines as well as men and Mark Gertler used the metaphor of the merry-go-round to speak of the appalling slaughter mechanised warfare had brought to the battlefield. The work of those artists and hundreds of other artist/soldiers established a tradition of war art which has been augmented and further expanded throughout the 20th century—a tradition which affirms that the purpose of war art is to condemn and expose the human suffering which war inflicts upon peoples.

In a sense all works of art inspired by war record a reaction to violence and to the destruction of human life. Many are made retrospectively and after long-term meditation on the nature of war and genocide. The intensified production of memorials, museums and public monuments towards the end of the 20th century concerns the preservation of memory. We live in a world in which the system of memory continually changes.

Remembrance as a source of energy needed to meet the challenges of the present and the future is implicit in the new public monuments to the Holocaust by Rachel Whiteread and Peter Eisenman in Vienna and in Berlin. In preserving the power of recollection which refuses to go away, art plays a significant role.

There are those who question whether it is possible or desirable for art to reflect upon and represent in any meaningful way memories of genocide and war. Adorno's cultural pessimism[1] and his statement that 'to write poetry after Auschwitz is barbaric' has been profoundly influential on the critical and theoretical discourse of the last 50 years. Adorno objected to the fact that the victims of genocide are made into something else, into so called works of art which are then tossed down for consumption by the very world which committed the act in the first place. For a great many artists however, there is no question that war is a legitimate and desirable subject of aesthetic reflection.

In an essay entitled *The artist as protester and commentator* T.G. Rosenthal[2] pointed out. 'As a group, artists are perhaps the most vocal and deeply committed sections of the population. It is possible, but not easy, to be a good painter and see the follies and cruelties of the world pass by without making at least a comment and at best a protest. The painting of a picture is an essentially private act yet, once painted, the picture becomes public because, if it is not seen and does not communicate its essence to others, it might as well not exist. This is never more true than in those paintings which have taken war as a theme, since in effect, the artist is addressing an audience far more directly than if he has painted a still life or a portrait.'

Joyce Cairns has spent the past decade and longer, painting about war. The series of paintings collectively entitled WAR TOURIST did not begin, however, in the manner of a carefully planned research project. War imagery in various guises surfaced in her work during the 1980s and in *Shadows of the Past* (1984) which the artist describes as her 'first war painting' it is made explicit. Again, in *They Said the War Partly was to Blame* (1986) unmistakable references to World War II (including her father in military uniform) play a prominent role. With *TV Dinners* (1991), we enter new territory. Painted in response to the Gulf War and dominated by elongated images of the artist absorbing the daily news bulletins on television, we realise that war as a subject has now become the central theme of Cairns' work. Over the next three years, *The Deadly Wars* (1993), *The Drums of War* (1993) and *Irma* (1994–95), were completed. All deal with the civil war in Bosnia. That atrocities such as 'ethnic cleansing' should happen in Europe in the late 20th century seemed unbelievable and many talked of feelings of helplessness as the terrible events in the Balkans unfolded. For Joyce Cairns there was only one possible response 'I had to paint a picture about Bosnia, the sheer horror of the situation, the plight of innocent civilians . . . the only way I can make a statement is through painting.'

Making paintings about war is no easy task. The complexity of the subject and how to interpret that complexity will always be problematic for artists. For Joyce Cairns, visiting battlefields, tracing the movements of armies and their victims, studying history and its artefacts, was only the beginning. The question of how best to use this material, to transform it into paintings which have meaning and relevance, not only for the artist but for others as well, still remained. In this context John Berger's[3] observation on how the painter makes visible what he sees is worth noting. 'The modern illusion concerning painting (which post-modernism has done nothing to correct) is that the artist is a creator. Rather he is a receiver. What seems like creation is the act of giving form to what he has received.'

Our ideas of war, and especially for those of us who fortunately have never participated in such actions, come chiefly from the cinema, television, photography and history books. Photography, from the American Civil War onwards, from Robert Capa to Don McCullin has offered an archive of images which for many will be definitive with regard to an understanding of the actuality of war and its consequences. Movie cameras were first used to record wars at the end of the 19th century and it is this kind of documentary reality (akin to the war photograph) which has fundamentally altered our perception of war. In *Rome, Open City* (1945) Roberto Rossellini, married documentary footage with studio scenes, changing forever our expectations with regard to codes of representation on the moving screen. Without a sense of the real—and this is true of any Hollywood blockbuster today as it is of any art film—it becomes impossible to take seriously any representation of war in the cinema.

Given the hierarchical authority of the photographic image or of filmed evidence, one wonders if the medium of painting can succeed in representing war. Leon Golub, who with his wife Nancy Spero, has over the past fifty years attacked the effects of military power and domination in their paintings of victimizers and victims, presented the case for painting as follows: 'I would put it this way, film or TV is the major force of visualization today. Every art form today has to be partially comprehended through a filmic dimension, our highly acute and compelled alertness to the time/motion dynamic. The static or passive become stop points or stressed situational locations counter to media and technological speed-ups. Painting is such a stop point. Painting, immobile, permits contemplation. Film is a fast medium; time is accelerated. Events telescope in film, freeze in painting. That crucifixion is metaphorically "there forever" in stopped time. In a world of electronic mega-transpositions, something that resists time, that stays still, can be of interest. In a fast moving world, that static quality of painting hasn't lost its force, perhaps it has greater or alternate force.'[4]

Joyce Cairns has always operated as a figurative painter with a story to tell. Insisting upon her own reality at all times, Cairns' constructed narratives were centred on what could be termed the autobiographical – the history of her family and an extensive examination of her own life provided an abundance of subject-matter. Her paintings of the 1970s and 1980s were passionately expressive, allowing her innermost thoughts full exposure on the canvas. Reality was combined with dreamlike and fantastic elements and invested her painting with an imaginative power capable of confronting and disturbing viewers. The centrality of personal experience which pervaded all of her work at this time (and is also found in the work of other women painters such as Frida Kahlo and Paula Rego) continues to underpin the war paintings of the past fifteen years.

As Cairns embarked upon the first of her war paintings it became clear that the subject of war would demand different modes of representation from her previous work. Her experiences of environments such as the North African desert and the former Nazi concentration camps, experiences both perplexing and fragmentary would need to be given coherence within a painting if the viewer is to decipher the complexity of imagery essential to the narrative. Cairns' methods of pictorial construction, which simultaneously balance the past and the present, the real with the imagined, the serious with the amusing, became more objective as the expressive gestures of her earlier paintings gave way to more considered compositional structures. Painting methods changed as well—with greater emphasis placed on drawing and colour applied more transparently than before. The significance of objects and their relationship to the battlefield becomes of paramount importance. In seeking a new combination of expression and precision in the representation of individual objects, Cairns fully understands that seeing a painting is very different from seeing an object, but without the accuracy of detail she invests in them, the meaning of the objects in her paintings would be diminished, as would the entire painting.

For Joyce Cairns, comprehension of war became meaningful through her imaginative identification with her father and his time in the British Army during World War II. Images of her father in army uniform had already appeared in paintings from the 1980s, but a decisive moment came when her elder brother presented her with a large suitcase containing all of her father's army papers and uniforms. Two paintings, both titled *Father's Memorabilia* (1995) depict the contents of the suitcase and encouraged Cairns to undertake several journeys—to Tunisia, to France, to Germany in order to trace her father's footsteps across various battlefields and to the places he had found himself in during the war. How Cairns approached this challenge, the questions she asked of herself as she made those journeys and how all of this developed into a larger discourse about the nature of war, is critical to the understanding of her war pictures.

In the paintings made after a visit to Tunisia in the Spring of 1995—*The Ghosts of Tunis* (1995–96), *Longstop Hill* (1995–96), *Mothers' Sons* (1996) and *War Tourist* (1998), Cairns consolidated her intentions with regard to the representation of her subject-matter. As she put it in relation to *The Ghosts of Tunis* 'everything in the painting exists, apart from the ghosts.' In other words, her dialogue with things seen and closely observed does not exclude the dreamlike or the exotic. Cairns describes *War Tourist* as 'a summary of all my war paintings at this time.' The invention of a major role for herself—that of a war tourist, not only places a strong female presence at the heart of all of the paintings, but also allows Cairns to act as an intermediary between the dead and the living, the past and the present. In *Longstop Hill,* the desert landscape provides a space which is filled with incident, including the artist and her father touring the battlefield on top of a camel —a sense of the whimsical permeates many of the works in the series. By way of contrast, *Mothers' Sons* is a sparse, solemn image showing Cairns sitting before the wall of a German cemetery, the balance between objective reality and personal experience movingly conveyed.

With regard to her father's wartime experiences, Cairns notes 'the majority of the men, my father included, had never been abroad. Arriving in Algeria and travelling into Tunisia must have been an incredible experience but one filled with fear and trepidation.' Although separated by fifty or so years, the Tunisian paintings bring to mind the opening lines of Hamish Henderson's *Elegies, For the Dead in Cyrenaica* first published in 1948[5].

> There are many dead in the brutish desert,
>   who lie uneasy
> among the scrub in this landscape of halfwit
> stunted ill-will. For the dead land is insatiate
> and necrophilous. The sand is blowing about still.
> Many who for various reasons, or because
>   of mere unanswerable compulsion, came here
> and fought among the clutching gravestones,
>   shivered and sweated,
> cried out, suffered thirst, were stoically silent, cursed
> the spittering machine-guns, were homesick for Europe
> and fast embedded in quicksand of Africa
>   agonized and died
> And sleep now. Sleep here the sleep of the dust.

Cairns' father was one of many Scots who fought in the desert and as well as Henderson, the poets Sorley Maclean, George Campbell Hay, Robert Garioch, G.S. Fraser and Edwin Morgan[6] all saw action in North Africa. Future overviews of Scottish cultural history will have greater opportunity to explore correspondences between Cairns' paintings and the poetry which emerged from the desert war.

Cairns visited Normandy in early 1996 and the resulting paintings, *Sword Beach* (1996) and *Normandy War Graves* (2005) provide further evidence of her mastery of big compositional structures. *Sword Beach* is the largest and most cinematic of the WAR TOURIST series—indeed it could be regarded as a mural painting with its powerful sense of both the epic and the panoramic. Again, the artist features as the main protagonist, pondering the events of history—events which not only changed the course of the world, but also shaped Cairns' own life. *Normandy War Graves* deploys much simpler compositional means. Her father and his dog, her brothers and sisters, as well as images of her younger and present day self are combined with a precisely recorded sense of place to create a gentle evocation of things past. The reality of *After the Battle* (1998) which suggests affinities with paintings of the Great War period was in fact reconstructed from material excavated from battlefields in Northern France and Belgium that Cairns had discovered in local museums. In the painting *In Flanders Fields* (2005) a sea of red poppies covers the entire surface symbolising the Ypres battlefield. The poppies are punctuated by various period artefacts, including an amputated hand placed in a surgical dish, all intended to represent fallen soldiers. For Cairns 'those surviving objects are the only way of keeping a tangible link to the past'.

Unimaginable, unspeakable, not representable. These are the words most often used in any discussion about what contribution the arts can make towards a culture of remembrance of the Holocaust. On the 50th anniversary of the liberation of Auschwitz, in January 1995, Neal Ascherson reflected upon these issues in an essay entitled *Remains of the Abomination*[7] 'Auschwitz is a symbol of many different things. But one of its best-understood meanings is about the contrast between life and machinery, between defenceless human bodies and the concrete and iron of the great industrial process put here to consume them. A million and a half people, more or less were killed here. The Nazis did not build the camp to last. The only solid part is the original nucleus, the rows of two-storey brick blocks which were once an Austro-Hungarian barracks and which the Germans took over from the defeated Polish Army in 1939. This was opened as a concentration camp in 1940. But then came the construction of Birkenau

(Auschwitz II), the gigantic wire enclosure a mile away which could hold 100,000 prisoners in wooden huts and which also contained the great industrial killing installation: a railway siding and unloading ramp, four purpose-built gas chambers, batteries of crematorium ovens . . . Since the war, Auschwitz has been a museum funded and administered by the Polish state. But no museum in the world has to face such problems of choice. What is to be done with this place?'[7]

That is a question which any artist attempting to make work about the Jewish Holocaust must also answer. Joyce Cairns visited the sites of Auschwitz and other former Nazi concentration camps on a journey to Germany, Poland and the Czech Republic in 1995. The resulting paintings, *Dark Shadows* (1996–97), *Polish Journey* (1998), *Auschwitz Memorial* (1999–2003) and *Shoes from Madjanek* (2002–05), were her response to this most problematic of subjects. The sombre atmosphere of *Dark Shadows* and *Polish Journey* is intended to express the menace and darkness of the concentration camps. The two main figures in *Dark Shadows* represent Jewish and Russian children—that both take on her likeness, perhaps reveals how strongly Cairns identifies with them. In *Polish Journey* painted as a memorial for the children of the Holocaust, Cairns creates a macabre stage-set, reminiscent of Kantor and his Cricot Theatre performances in the prominence given to the dolls, lit candles, and objects from Auschwitz, Madjanek and Terezín.

'The only way I could give back status, respect and acknowledgement of the desperate suffering and dehumanisation, was through the medium of portraiture: I know their faces so well that they still haunt my sleep.' The photographs of the inmates and victims which today line the corridors of the buildings in Auschwitz became the source material for *Auschwitz Memorial*, the largest and most austere of Cairns' Holocaust paintings. This painting and its companion, *Shoes from Madjanek* took three to four years to complete, a testament to the immense effort needed to portray those faces and shoes. 'The concentration camp at Madjanek is very chilling, the barrack construction rough and primitive. There were two or three huts filled solidly with rotting shoes crammed into large cages. The smell of the decaying rubber was overwhelming.' For Cairns the activation and expression of memories which have long been erased from consciousness is an important part of the artist's task. Only by doing so, can art, by means of the power of shared experience, find ways of dealing with the great tragedies of our time.

In addition to the 'big statements' of the large paintings, a complementary group of smaller pictures take us home, as it were to

Footdee, the harbour village where Cairns has lived for many years. In both *Messerschmitt over Footdee* (2003) and *The Anderson Shelter* (2004), the North Sea looms in the background. Once again past and present merge together as Cairns imagines a German bomber coming in over the sea and her mother in the shelter—both she and her brother were of course born after the war ended. In *Pusser's Rum* (2002) and *Bonjour Field Marshall* (2002) the artist is again seen centre-stage, standing in her own life, surrounded by smaller images and objects. Cairns invests all of those works with a haunting, dreamlike quality where a sense of intimate contact with her past is all-prevailing.

In appraising the war paintings of Joyce Cairns it is worth reminding ourselves that few significant images of war emerged in Scottish art during both World Wars and that afterwards the dominant tradition of painterly colourism appeared to preclude war as a suitable subject. During the 1960s, however, a series of paintings by William Crozier of skeletal figures placed in barren landscapes reflected his preoccupation at that time with the victims of the concentration camps. 'The image of man in the 20th century will not be the cinema stars or pop idols, but the victims of Belsen.'[8] John Bellany, after a visit to the former concentration camp of Buchenwald in 1967, made a number of paintings depicting camp inmates alongside Vietnamese women and children linking the victims of the Holocaust with the war in Vietnam and protesting against the evil of war. More recently, Peter Howson (who briefly served in the British Army and who also worked as an 'official' war artist in Sarajevo) and Ken Currie have made paintings concerning war and atrocity in response to the violent events happening throughout the world. It could be said that Crozier and Bellany presented us with expressionist visions of hell while Howson and Currie showed us the world as a Brueghelesque lunatic asylum.

In addressing the question of war, Joyce Cairns offers us a very different interpretation —an interpretation which began with memories of childhood, but gradually took on a resonance larger than any autobiographical or local predicament. Sixty years after World War II, Cairns has created her own sequence of 'heroic elegies'—her own deeply felt meditations on the nature of war.

Much has been made of the marginalisation of women artists in recent histories of art, but this does not seem to have prevented Joyce Cairns from overcoming whatever difficulties placed in her path. Long recognised as one of the leading painters of her generation, she has always brought a strong, independent, modern woman's perspective to everything she does as an artist. THE WAR TOURIST paintings are the culmination of many years of searching and thinking. They look back to her earlier investigations of narrative and self and forward to an engagement with new and demanding subject-matter. Growing up in the shadow of World War II and its subsequent effect on her childhood has ultimately led Cairns to take on the subject of war. By fearlessly rising to this challenge she has demonstrated that painting remains a contemporary art form fully capable of representing the traumatic events of war. In doing so, she has made a very special and unique contribution to the story of Scottish Art.

[1] Adorno, Theodor W.
Prisms: A Critique of Culture and Society, 1955
Adorno also states (in *Negative Dialectics*) that 'Auschwitz has proved beyond doubt that culture has failed ... after Auschwitz all culture, and that includes even the deliberate criticism of it, is rubbish'. Adorno knew of course that art would continue to exist—but not only art—even concentration camps would continue to exist.

[2] Rosenthal, T.G.
The artist as protestor and commentator from
The Artist and War in the 20th Century,
BBC Publications, 1967

[3] Berger, John
'Steps Towards a Small Theory of the Visible' from *The Shape of a Pocket*,
Bloombury, 2001

[4] Golub, Leon
Do Paintings Bite?
Selected Texts 1948–96
Cantz Verlag, 1997

[5] Henderson, Hamish
Elegies For the Dead in Cyrenaica
The 1977 edition (EUSPB Edinburgh) contains an introduction by Sorley MacLean who comments:
'The book is thus the work of a man concerned not only with contemplating and recording a momentous piece of the world's history, but also with changing the world, even if it sees the war of 1939–45 not so much as action to change the world for the better, but to prevent its change for the worse.'

[6] Morgan, Edwin
Sonnets from Scotland, 1984
In the poem entitled 'North Africa' Morgan's opening line asks 'why did the poets come to the desert?'
He then proceeds to make reference to Henderson, MacLean, Garioch, Campbell Hay and G.S. Fraser and well as himself.

[7] Ascherson, Neal
Remains of the Abomination
THE INDEPENDENT ON SUNDAY
22 January 1995
Ascherson also noted 'Time cannot be imprisoned. When I first visited Auschwitz more than 30 years ago, I could pull up the turf anywhere in the open ground beyond the end of the railway track and find the earth white-ish: a paste of calcinated human bone and ash. Now, the carbon cycle has quietly done its work over half a century, and the soil is brown again.'

[8] Crozier, William
Paintings and Drawings 1951–85
MacLaurin Art Gallery Ayr, 1985
Quoted in the Catalogue Introduction by Katharine Crouan

Joyce Cairns
All quotations in the text are taken from a series of notes on the paintings which the artist sent to the writer after a discussion in the artist's studio in August 2005.

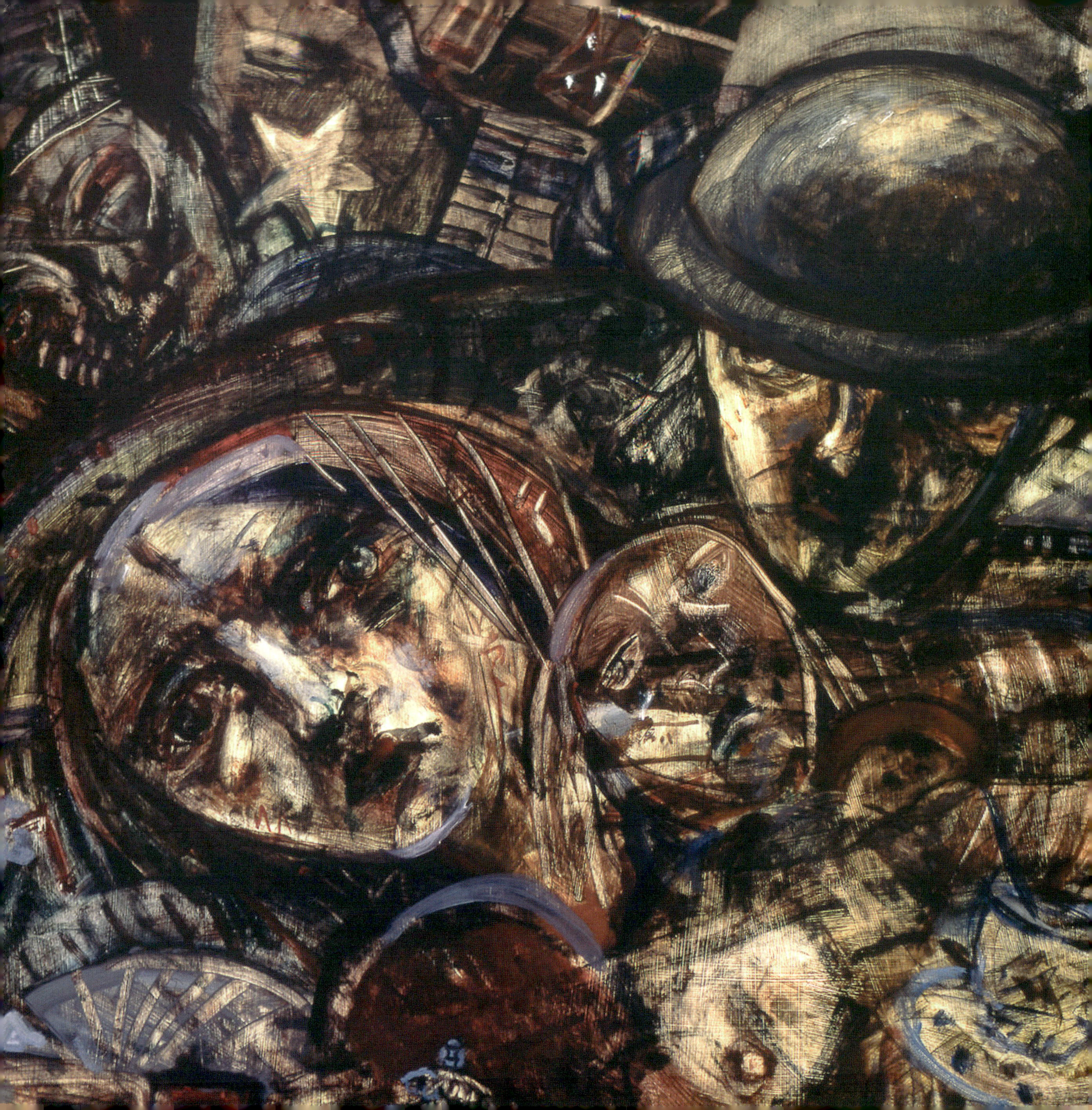

A FIRST RESPONSE

After my mother died in March 1983 the group of paintings which followed was both introspective and reflective. Her death and the clearing of her house made me think again about my father who had died in 1972.

PLATE FOUR

Shadows of the Past,
Liberation Ceremony, Rennes, 1984
Oil on panel. 183 × 244 cm

FROM THE SCOTTISH ARTS COUNCIL COLLECTION
BEQUEATHED TO HIGHLAND COUNCIL

Photograph © Ewen Weatherspoon

My first war painting.

When on holiday in Brittany in 1984, I witnessed the celebration of the fortieth anniversary of the liberation of Rennes. I saw the allied flags fly over groups of war veterans marching through the town and with the realisation that my father too had fought in France, a seed was sown.

In this painting the female figure could be seen as France, despoiled by invaders; the teapot, cup and saucer came from my mother, and the German offering cakes suggests collaboration and temptation. Initially research was flimsy; I think I may have bought some war comics to inform the detailing of the uniforms.

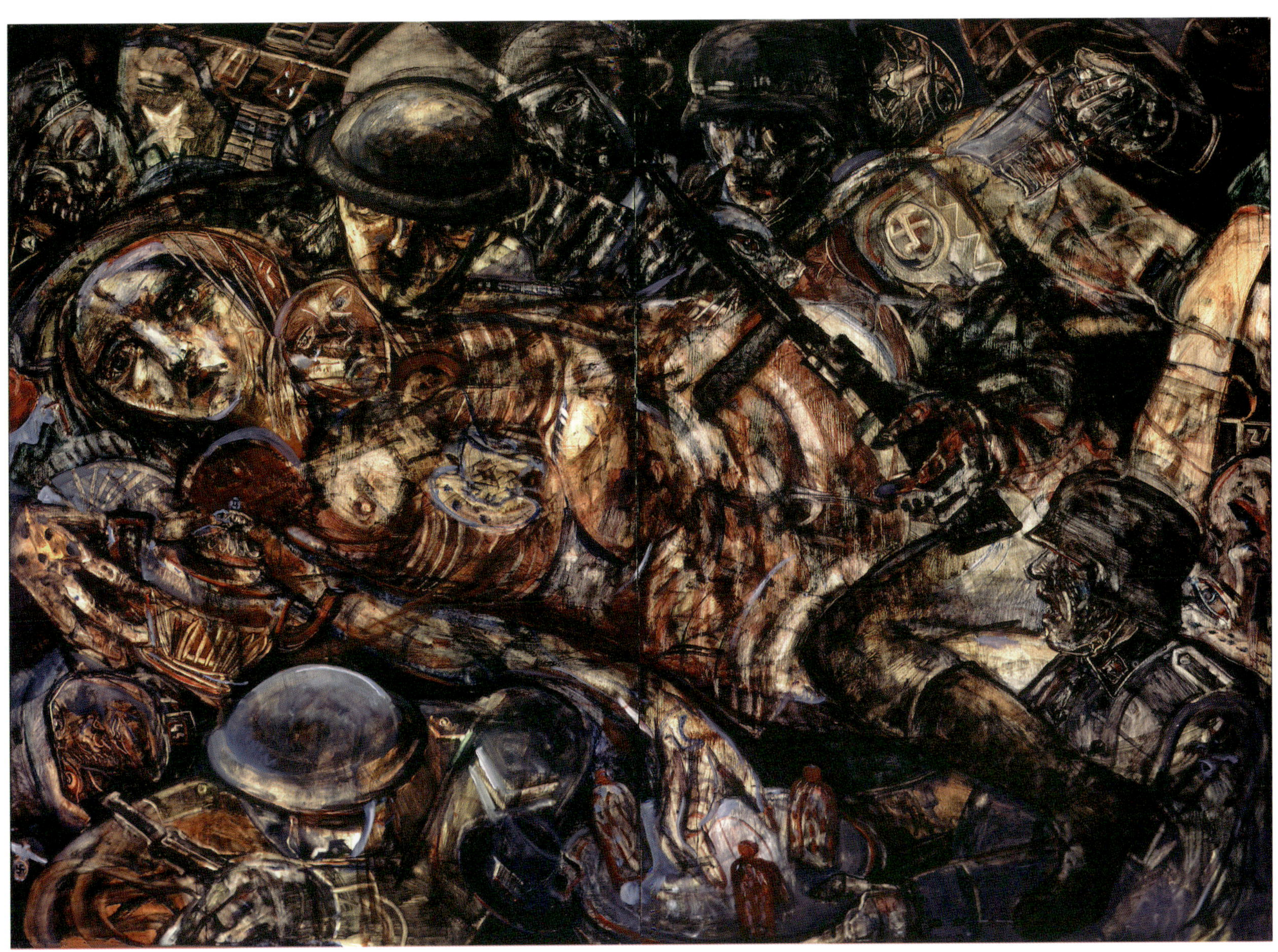

PLATE FIVE

War Games, 1986

Oil on panel, 122 x 213cm

CITY ARTS CENTRE:
CITY OF EDINBURGH MUSEUMS AND GALLERIES

Photograph © Antonia Reeve

Over the next two years my interest in war slowly developed, but initially it was more centred on the nautical due, perhaps, to my living by the sea. From the Sea Cadet Headquarters behind my house the Unit marches up and down Pocra Quay and also hosts functions to which the village is invited. Naval boats from Britain and abroad come into the harbour and have open days which I always used to attend with my camera—finding new images to enrich the work, adding to its authenticity. In 1985 I visited for the first time, The Imperial War Museum, The Chelsea Army Museum and HMS Belfast.

In this painting Camel cigarettes and a rum bottle are set out on the table where major decisions are being made at the flick of a Tarot card. A test missile from HMS Galatea and the bell from Aberdeen's North Pier Lighthouse show the start of my interest in the artefact as a key element within a narrative.

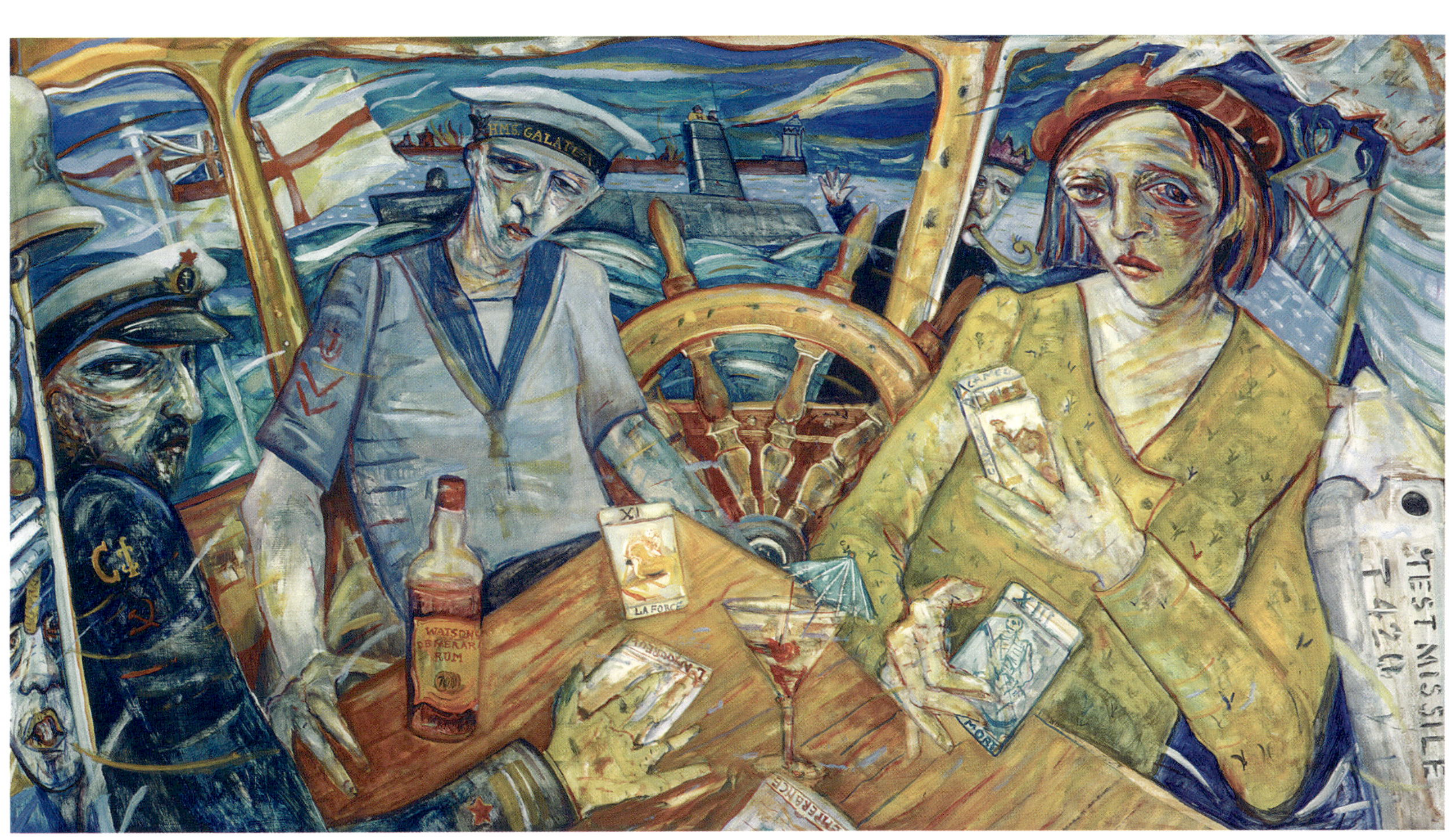
HMS. GALATEA
XI
LA FORCE
RUM
XIII
TEST MISSILE
T 420

PLATE SIX

They Said the War was Partly to Blame, 1986
Oil on panel, 213 x 244 cm

A family psychodrama. Set partly in the bathroom at Dovecote Grove in Edinburgh when I was about nine years old, my mother stands at the wash-hand basin while I look back through time from Footdee and its war memorial. There are seven family toothbrushes inscribed with our names and the school children are my younger brother and me with Peter Rabbit, I am also shown as a nurse at The Western General Hospital where I worked in 1966. The tilted green tiled floor has some spots of blood that never came off, testimony to a trauma that was never discussed. My father looks through the boat windows, past a parrot given to me by my students.

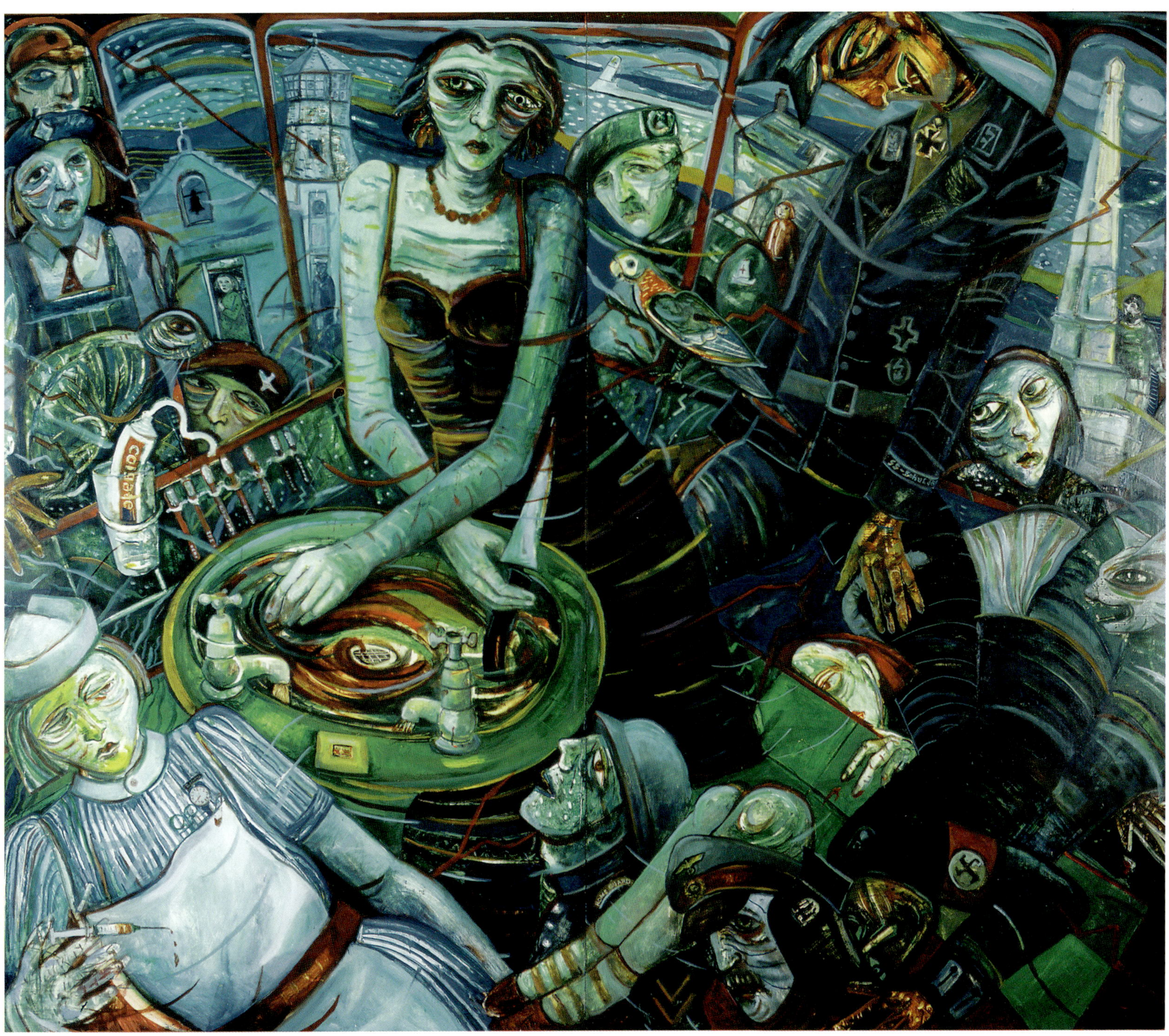
Colgate

PLATE SEVEN

TV Dinners, 1991

Oil on panel, 213 x 244 cm

GLASGOW CITY COUNCIL
(MUSEUMS)

The Gulf War of 1991 was the first real televised war and, like the majority of the population, I watched the battles unfold minute by minute through almost continuous news coverage. I ate every meal in front of the television and developed a less than healthy interest in the jingoistic reporting of tabloid newspapers. A T-shirt advertised in the Daily Star was emblazoned with American and British flags, under which was written 'These colours don't run'. Much reporting was focused on body bags and hero-worship was directed at 'top gun' pilots. The Falklands War, though televised, had been more heavily censored and mainly reported after the event.

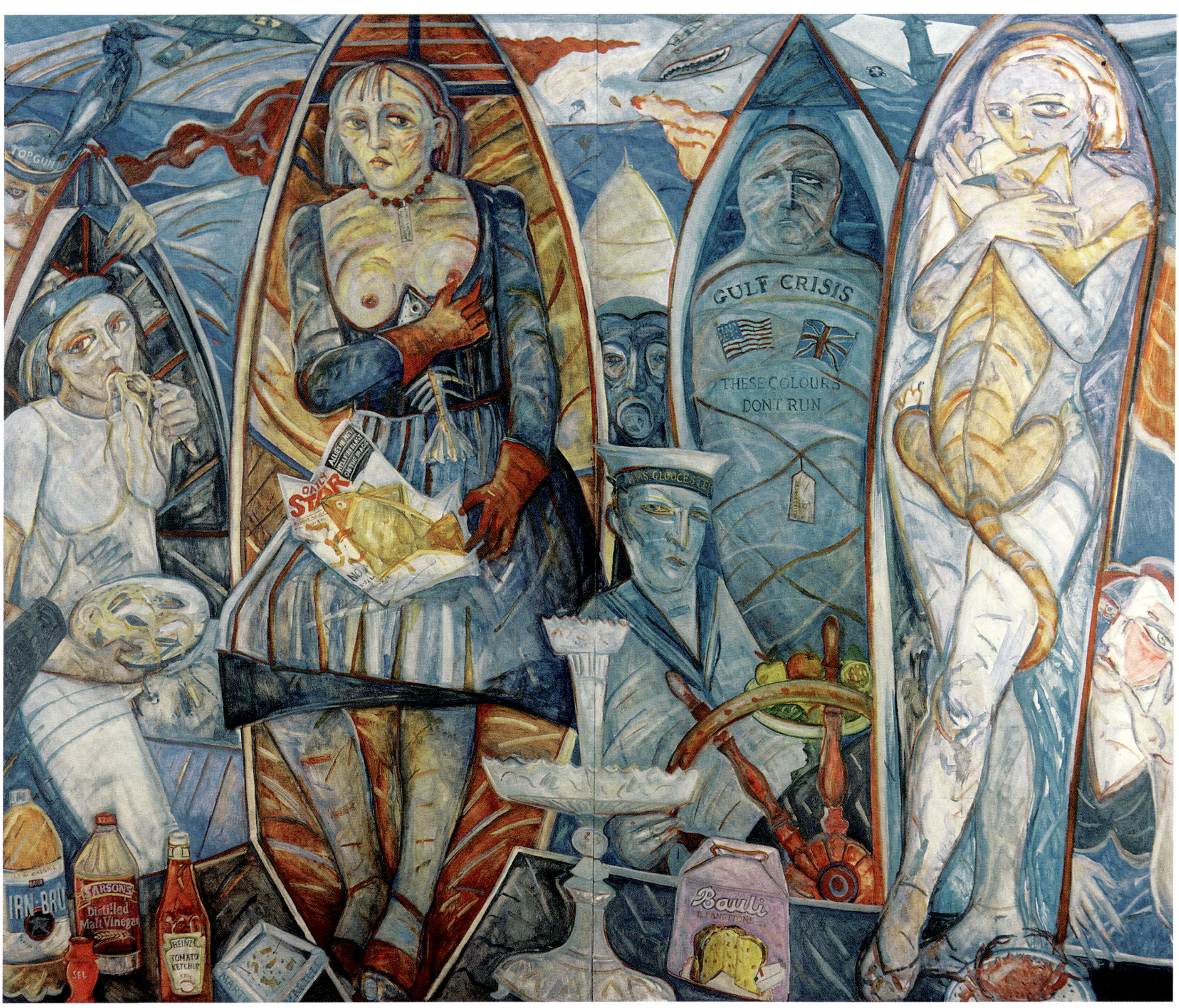
TOP GUN
GULF CRISIS
THESE COLOURS
DON'T RUN
STAR
IRN-BRU
SARSONS
Distilled
Malt Vinegar
HEINZ
TOMATO
KETCHUP
SEL
Bauli
IL PANETTONE

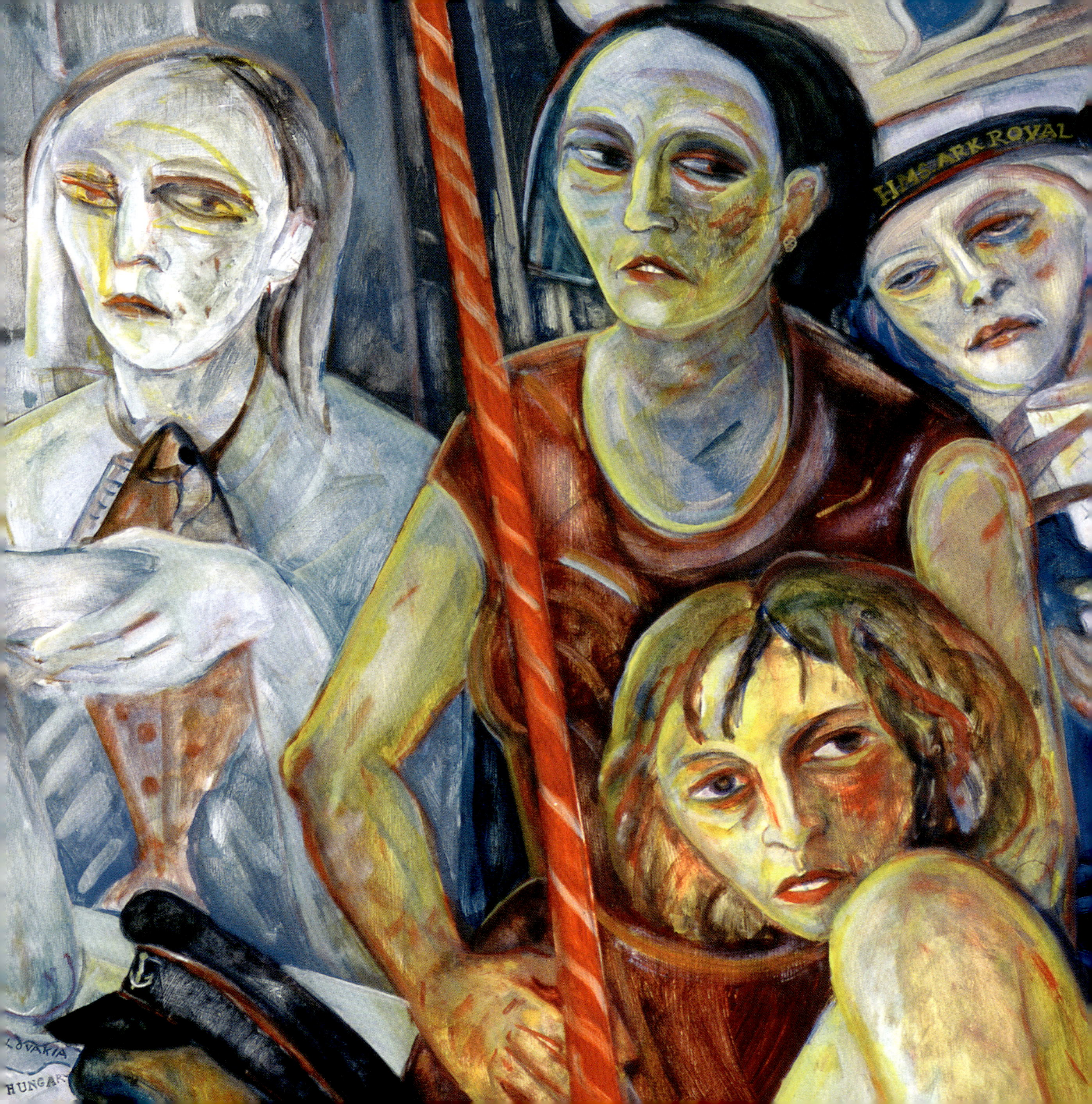
H.M.S. ARK ROYAL
LOVAKIA
HUNGAR

THE BOSNIAN SUITE

THE BOSNIAN WAR, from 1992 to 1994, was the result of centuries of religious and ethnic tensions which erupted after Tito's death. It occurred in an area which we considered to be almost European and it was shocking to think, while sipping a Bellini in Harry's Bar in Venice, that just across the Adriatic genocide was once again occurring. No-one could have foreseen this almost fifty years ago when, at the end of the Second World War, the concentration camps were being liberated.

The tragedy unfolding through the media was there for all to witness and I was not alone in my distaste for the bumbling of the UN and NATO. This conflict, which resulted in the murder, rape and mutilation of so many Bosnian Muslims, could have been defused before it escalated out of control. Over two hundred thousand Bosnians were killed and several hundred thousand driven from their homes, many of which were then ransacked and destroyed. It would appear that there is still no effective international policy to deal with ethnic genocide, as witnessed in Rwanda, Kosovo and East Timor.

PLATE EIGHT

The Drums of War, 1993
Oil on panel, 183 x 122 cm

Based on a news item about a Muslim family, mainly women and children, who were burned to death in the cellar of their home by the Serbs. The blackened hand holds a UN badge, assigning blame for the continuing slaughter. The caged hens symbolise the inevitable victims.

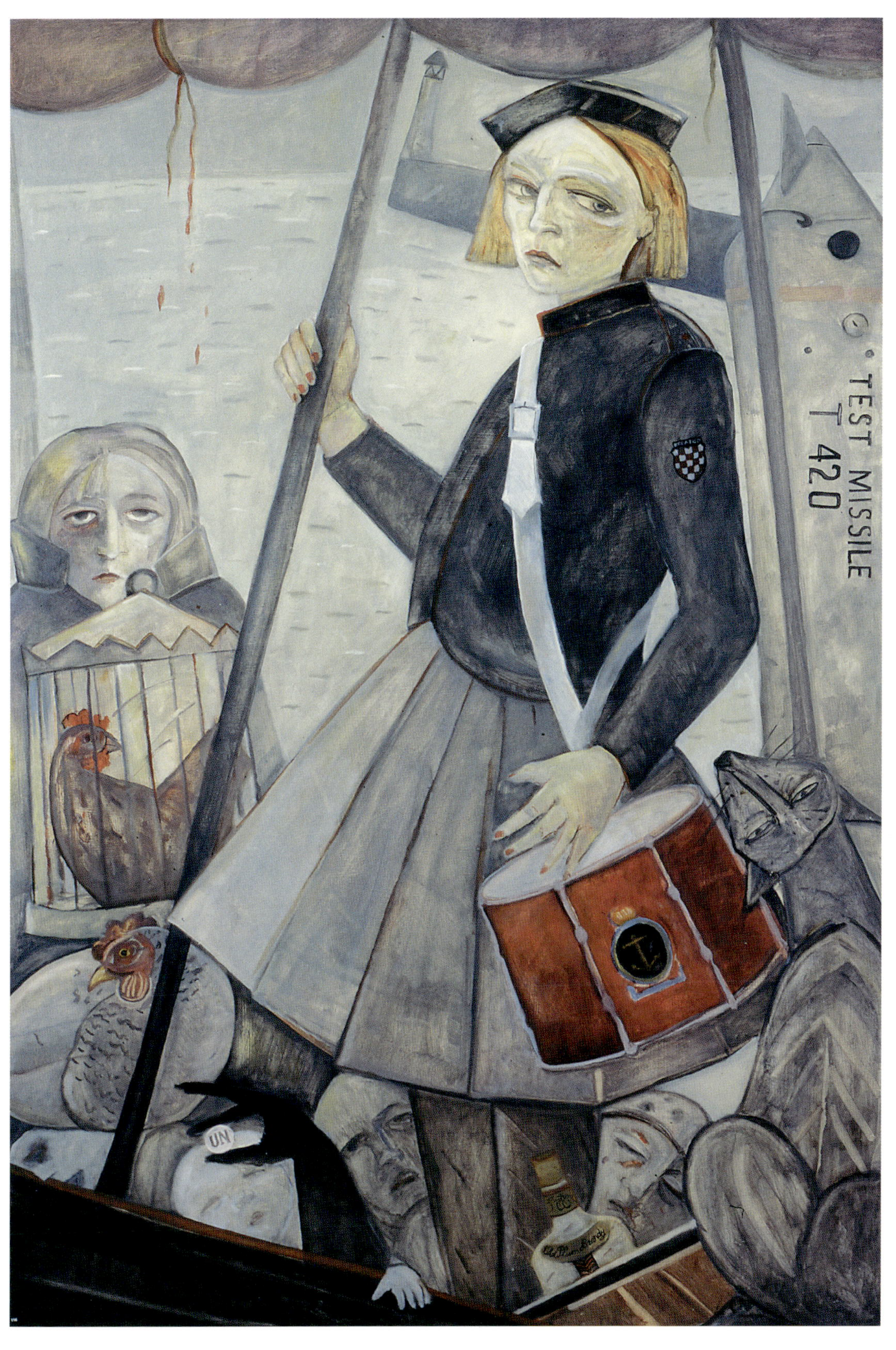
TEST MISSILE
T 420
UN

PLATE NINE

The Deadly Wars, 1993

Oil on panels, 213 x 244 cm

PERTH MUSEUM AND ART GALLERY,
PERTH AND KINROSS COUNCIL, SCOTLAND

Reproduced by permission of
Perth Museum and Art Gallery,
Perth and Kinross Council, Scotland

For the deadly wars are blast and blawn,
An gentle peace returnin,
It left monys the bairnie faitherless,
An monys a widow mournin.

From the singing of
Jeannie Robertson,
Aberdeen

I felt that I had to paint this picture about Bosnia—the horror of the situation, the plight of an innocent population and my anger over the inability of the Western powers to find a realistic solution. The only way I could have made a statement with any degree of eloquence was through painting.

Three years earlier I had photographed an old merry-go-round in La Rochelle, one with cockerels and rabbits as well as the more usual horses and later I saw another at La Defense in Paris, with cats and pigs. From the start I thought the continuous circling of the carousel could be a symbol for all wars, but it took three years from the initial thought to the completion of the picture. The three figures riding at odds with one another are a Croatian, a Muslim and a Serb, while I observe as a ghostly presence.

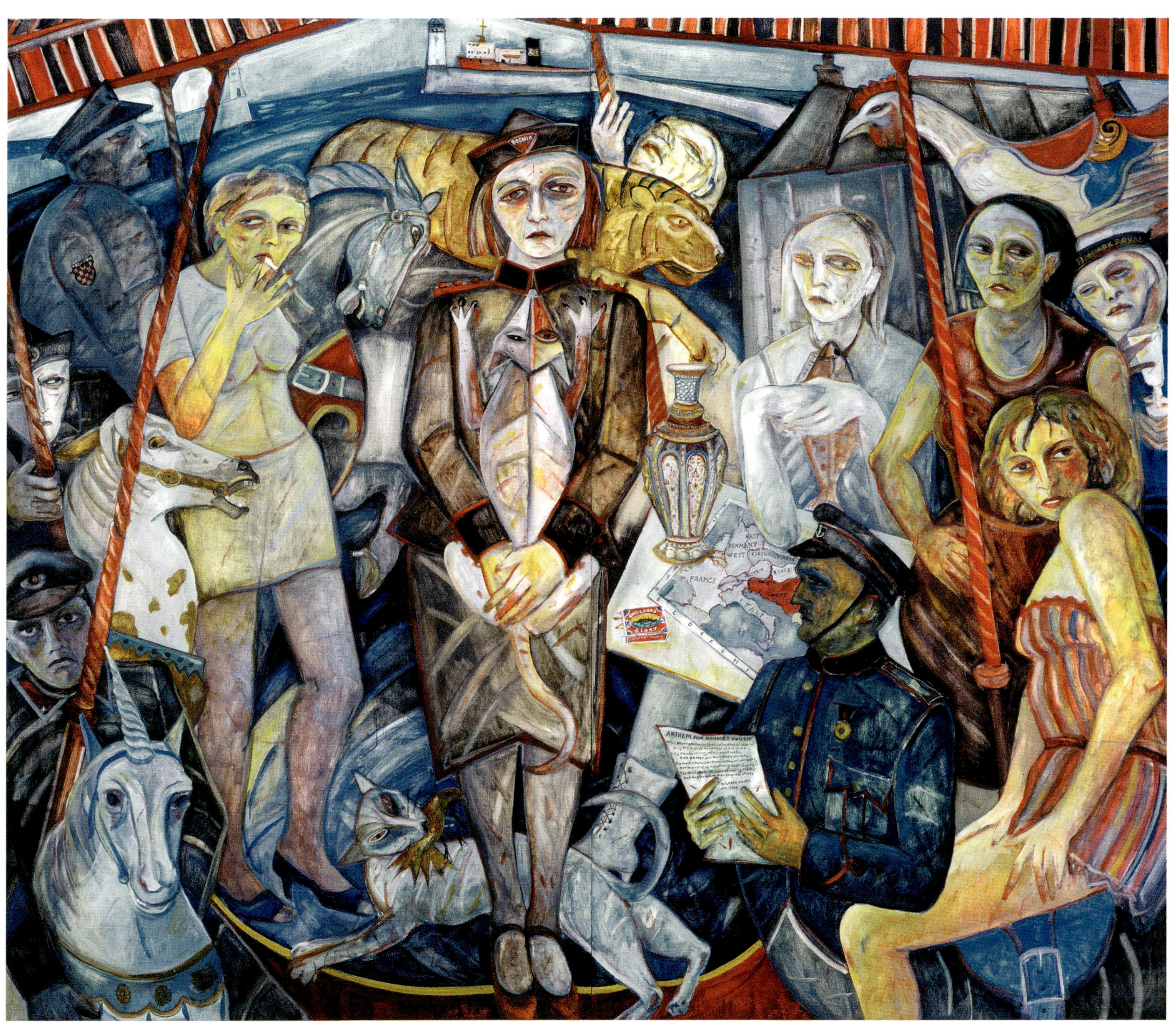
BOSNIA
HMS ARK ROYAL
EAST
GERMANY
WEST
FRANCE
AUSTRIA
HUNGARY
ITALY
ENGLAND'S GLORY
ANTHEM FOR DOOMED YOUTH
WILFRED OWEN

PLATE TEN

Irma, 1994–95

Oil on panels, 213 x 244 cm

Irma Hadzimuratovic, a seven year old Bosnian girl, was airlifted from Sarajevo to Britain after receiving severe injuries in the mortar attack which killed her mother. Supported by a public appeal she arrived in Britain on September 11, 1993 having been paralysed from the neck down. She spent the rest of her short life on a ventilator, eventually dying here on April 1, 1995.

I painted Irma as a tribute, thinking that she might like the merry-go-round despite the sinister meaning I had given to it, but she had died before the picture was completed.

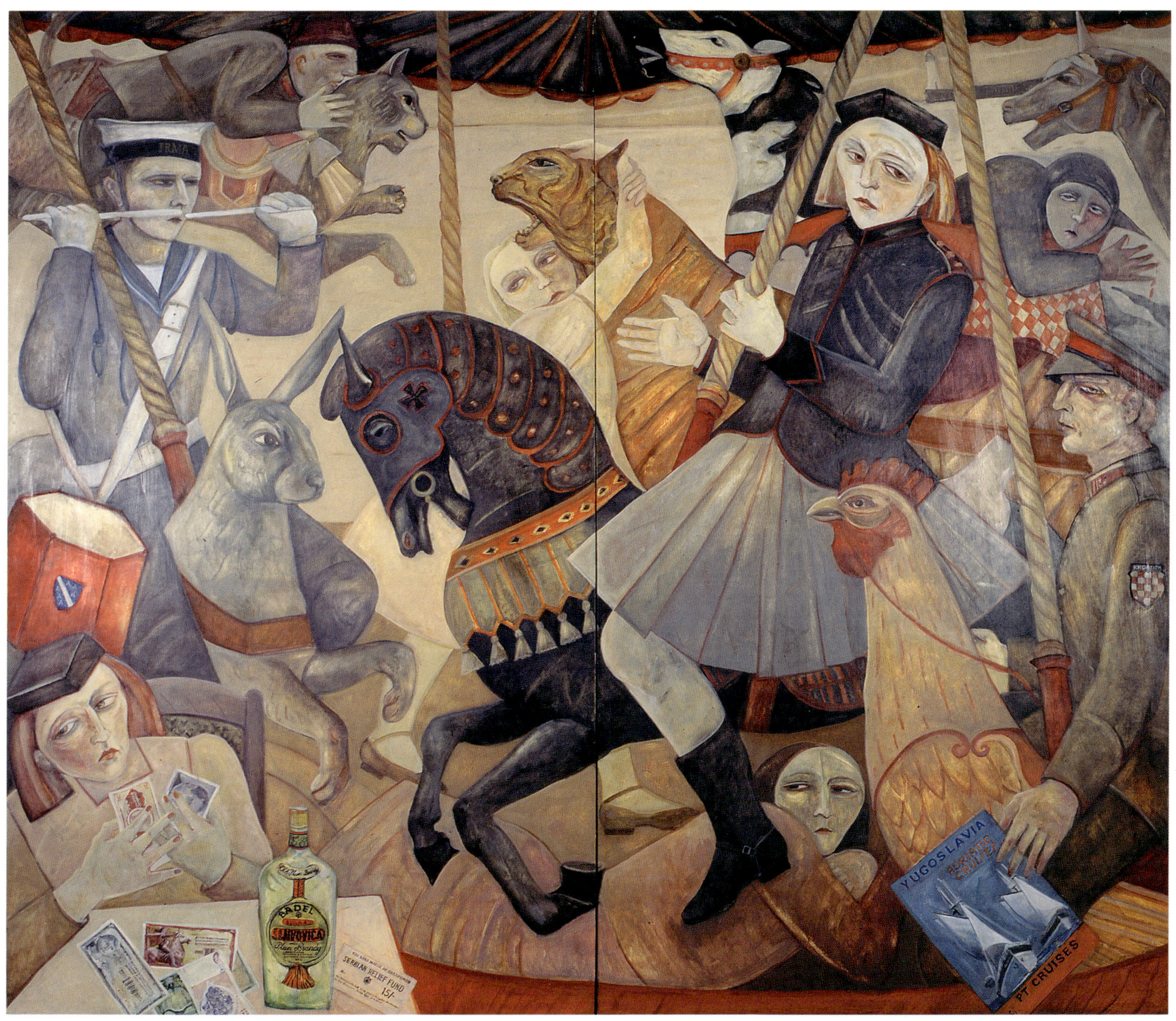
IRMA
BADEL
Plum Brandy
SERBIAN RELIEF FUND
15/-
YUGOSLAVIA
ADRIATIC CRUISES
PT CRUISES

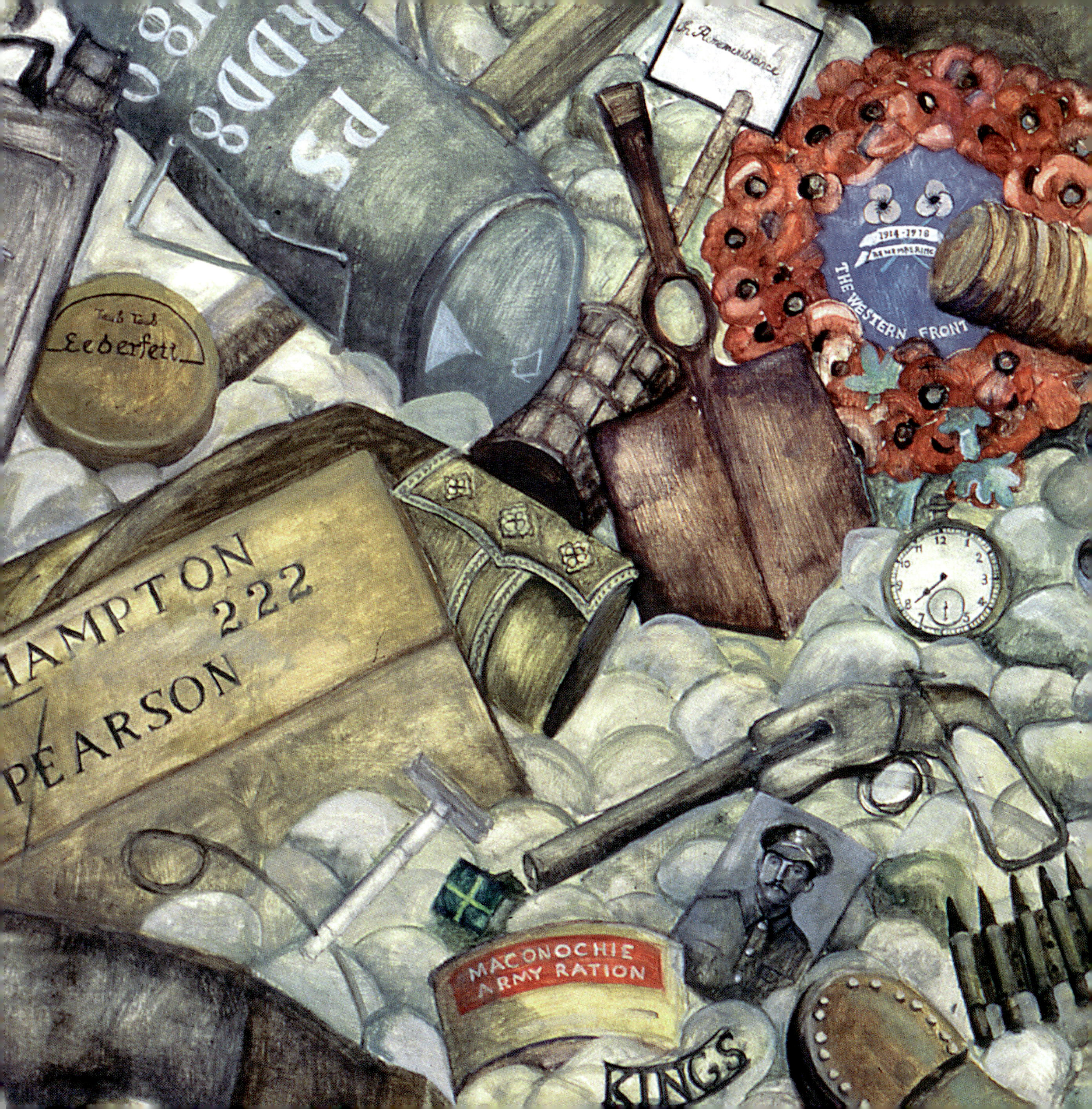
PS
In Remembrance
1914-1918
THE WESTERN FRONT
HAMPTON
222
PEARSON
MACONOCHIE
ARMY RATION
KINGS

THE FIRST WORLD WAR

What passing bells for those who die as cattle?
Only the monstrous anger of the guns,
Only the stuttering rifles' rapid rattle
Can patter out their hasty orisons.
No mockeries for them from prayers or bells.
Nor any voice of mourning save the choirs,—
The shrill, demented choirs of wailing shells;
And bugles calling for them from sad shires.

Anthem for Doomed Youth by WILFRED OWEN

MOST YEARS we drive from Zeebrugge to south-east France. It is impossible to travel through Belgium and northern France without being aware of the scattered memorials and graves glimpsed through fields and trees. Signposts reveal place-names that are synonymous with grief and destruction focusing the memory on the unprecedented casualties from 'the war to end all wars'.

Over the years we have often stopped for a couple of nights in Arras, Cambrai, Reims or Ypres. We visit museums and pay our respects to those who lie in the acres upon acres of military cemeteries sited where the fighting took place.

In 1995 I enrolled on my first battlefield tour, 'The Battlefields of the Great War' run by Milestone Tours and organised with military precision. Information came from the tour guide interspersed with bursts of such topical music as 'Hang out your washing on the Siegfried Line'. Fellow travellers included war veterans, those wishing to find the graves of relatives and others, like myself, who had a genuine interest in the war and wished to see at first-hand where history had been made.

In Ypres, you could buy chocolate helmets and dark greyish-green candles formed as portrait busts of a British Tommy, yet to light one now would seem almost sacrilegious.

PLATE ELEVEN

After the Battle, 1996

Oil on panels, 213 x 244 cm

This work contrasts the detritus of mechanised warfare with the intimate personal belongings that linked combatants with their families at home, only possible through extensive research in a range of museums and libraries—for example I have appropriated the shafts of light from the shell blast in *The Ypres Salient at Night*, by Paul Nash.

In the Hotel Beatus in Cambrai, Madame's son, Phillippe Gorczynski, who is an expert on the battle of Cambrai has for some years been excavating tank parts from the battlefield and delighted in showing us his rusting collection. Since our visit he has found a badly damaged but complete D47 tank, 'Deborah'. He may know the location of two more and hopes to have 'Deborah' on display at Flesquieres as a monument to the memory of soldiers who died at Cambrai. Phillippe very kindly arranged for us to visit the former mayor of Bullecourt, Jean Letaille, who has his own private museum of World War One memorabilia and many of the items in *After the Battle* came from this source. Other objects came from the relatively new museum set up in the old fort at Peronne and also the Musée d'Abris, in the underground caverns at Albert, the Flanders Field Museum at Ypres and The Imperial War Museum in London.

The location, created from photographs I took in Sanctuary Wood, shows the original trench systems still in place, complete with duckboards and mud. The museum there has a random selection of decaying items crammed together in old-fashioned cases along with a great many stereoscopic machines where, by turning a handle, one can see amazing 3-D images of the war, many quite gruesome. Through use, these glass plates are becoming scratched and may soon be lost forever.

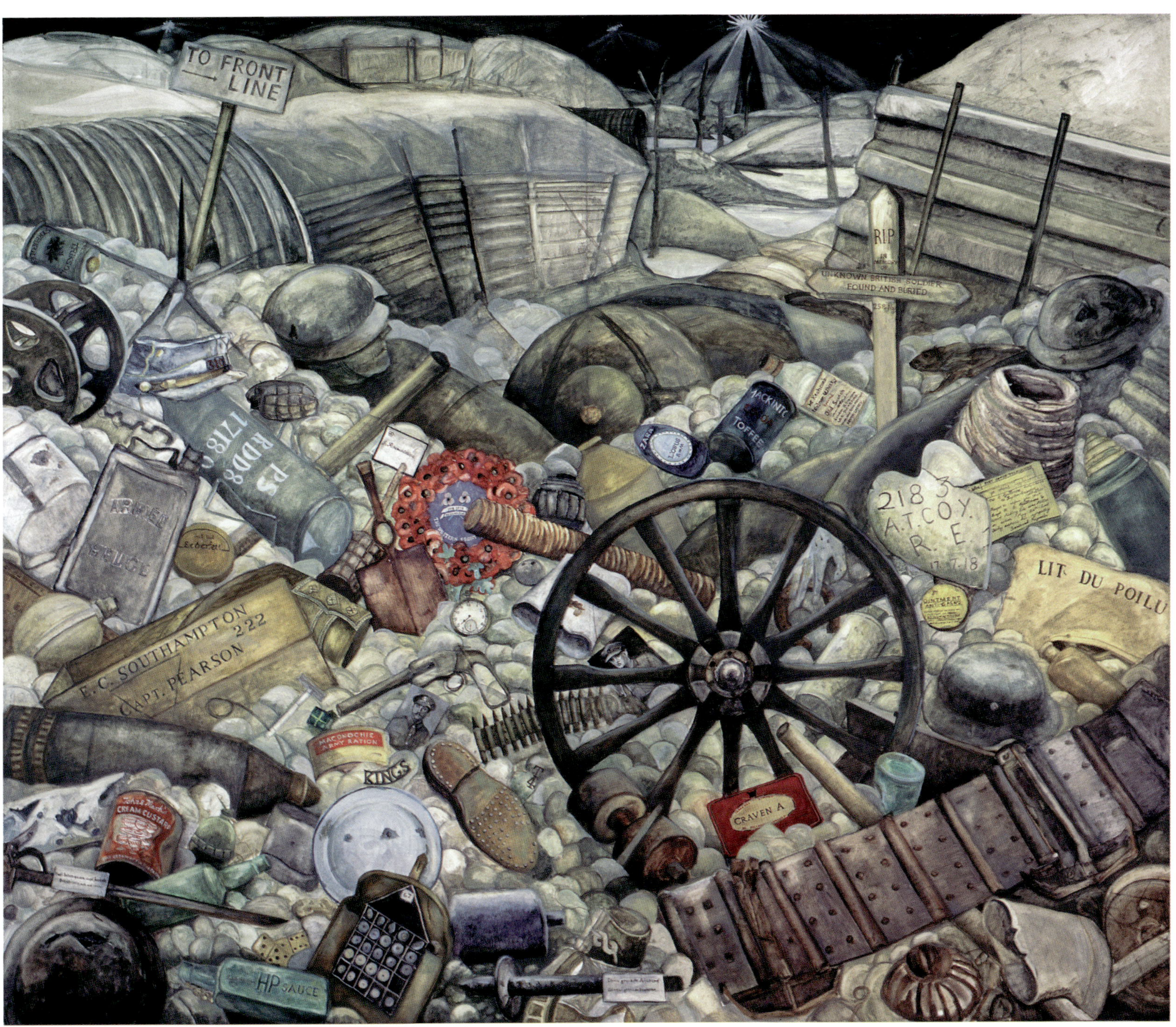

TO FRONT LINE
R.I.P.
UNKNOWN BRITISH SOLDIER
FOUND AND BURIED
TOFFEE
PS
RDD8
1718
2183
A.T.CO.Y.
R. E
17.7.18
LIT DU POILU
E.C. SOUTHAMPTON
222
CAPT. PEARSON
MACONOCHIE
ARMY RATION
KINGS
CRAVEN A
CREAM CUSTARD
HP SAUCE

In Flanders Fields

In Flanders fields the poppies blow
Between the crosses, row on row,
That mark our place; and in the sky
The larks, still bravely singing, fly
Scarce heard amid the guns below.
We are the Dead, Short days ago
We lived, fell down, saw sunset glow,
Loved and were loved, and now we lie
in Flanders fields.

John McCrae 1915

PLATE TWELVE

In Flanders Fields, 2005

Oil on panels, 213 x 244 cm

These lines were the initial inspiration for the painting. After three solid days treating the wounded, Lieutenant Colonel John McCrae of the Royal Canadian Army Medical Corps. stumbled out of the underground dressing station at Essex Farm to see poppies growing on the broken ground. Many soldiers on the Western Front believed that these poppies had been nurtured by the blood of the fallen. The Times published a powerful photograph of a blind craftsman making a wreath, surrounded by a sea of paper poppies and that image, along with the poem, gave me the reason to laboriously paint all these poppies as a mark of respect for the endurance of those soldiers so long dead.

Nearly ten million men died in the Great War. Of the seven hundred and fifty thousand British soldiers, sailors and airmen who died on the Western Front, over three hundred thousand have no known grave. In my mind, they lie underneath this field of poppies on which are scattered artefacts which would have been familiar to the combatants. The painting includes some of the brands and packaging which reflected sentiments prevalent during that war, like Campaign Assorted Biscuits and Tipperary Toffee. Lord Kitchener was transformed into a doll for more affluent children. The 'terror' tank first used on the Somme in 1916 could crash through barbed wire entanglements and over trenches became such a symbol of success that it was used as the model for a bank for the tank savings scheme. War adventure books and patriotic games such as *The Great European War*, *The Race for Berlin* and *Running the Blockade*, were all part of an ongoing campaign to alert the civilian population to the reality of the war

These artefacts became synonymous with the human condition and, as they do in other paintings, build memory and remembrance. The colour of the poppies is vibrant and deceptively positive but reality is closer to the rat, the mills bomb (from my own collection) and the kidney dish with a severed, gangrenous hand, crawling with bluebottles. The helmets, which in life had rendered their wearers anonymous, now suggest the anonymity of the dead.

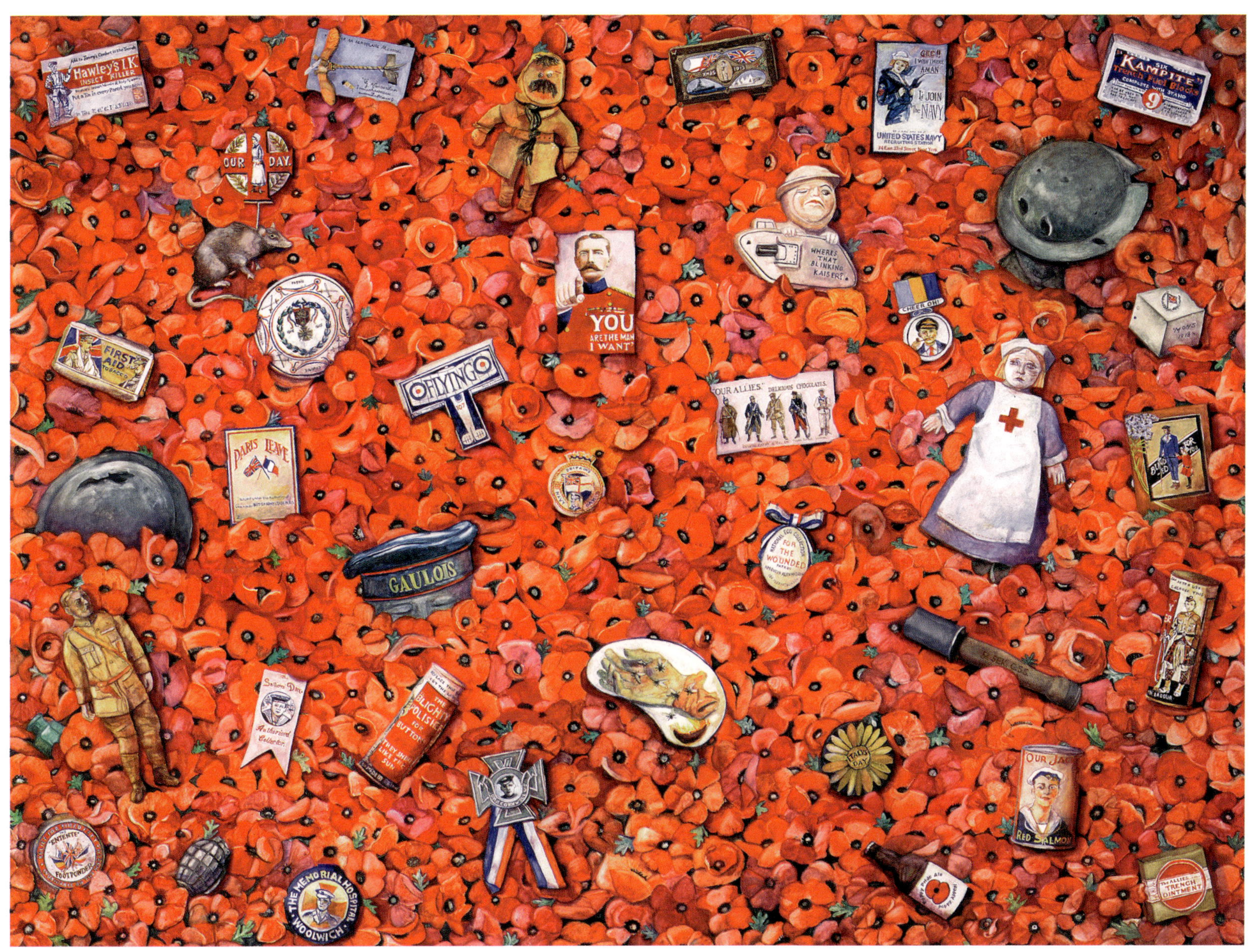

Hawley's I.K.
INSECT KILLER
OUR DAY
SIX
KAMPITE
Trench Fuel Blocks
9
GEE!! I WISH I WERE A MAN
I'd JOIN THE NAVY
UNITED STATES NAVY
WHERES THAT BLINKING KAISER?
YOU
ARE THE MAN I WANT
CHEER OH!
FIRST AID TOBACCO
FLYING
"OUR ALLIES" DELICIOUS CHOCOLATES
PARIS LEAVE
FOR THE WOUNDED
GAULOIS
ENTENTE
FOOT POWDER
THE MEMORIAL HOSPITAL WOOLWICH
ITALY'S DAY
OUR JACK
RED SALMON
THE ALLIES TRENCH OINTMENT

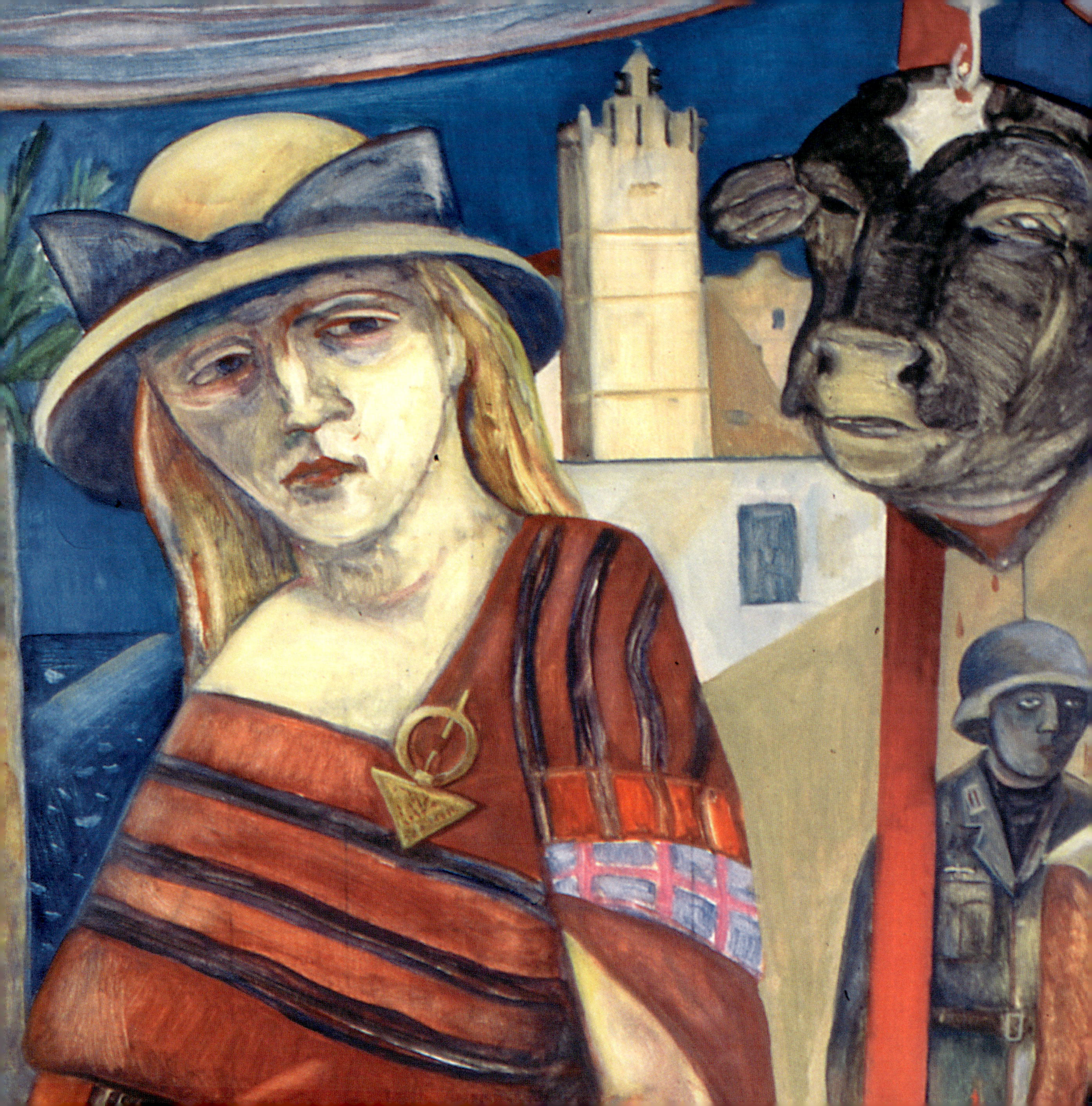

MY FATHER'S WAR

We visited Tunisia in the spring of 1995, flying to Tunis and hiring a car so that we could explore the areas where fighting took place. Tunisia, 'The Granary of the Roman Empire', is a country of enormous contrasts and beauty where Romans, Vandals, Byzantines, Spaniards, Turks and latterly the French all left their traces. Tunis and parts of Sousse have a European flavour, with colonial French architecture and boulevards where signage is in both French and Arabic. Once outside the coastal resorts you step back in time, with few changes since my father was here in 1942–43.

Driving along the narrow roads, one passes donkey carts, while sheep and goats stare out from the back of open trucks. The countryside can change dramatically—rich agricultural farmland covered in olive groves in the Mejerda Valley, dried up wadis, cactus and scrubland where camels wander freely along the roadside, and rugged mountains rise from the plains. This countryside has many Roman remains, most in a remarkable state of preservation like those at Dougga and the large amphitheatre at El Jem which has names, towns and dates incised in the ancient walls by American soldiers from World War Two.

PLATE THIRTEEN

The Ghosts of Tunis, 1995–96

Oil on panels, 213 x 244 cm

The Ghosts of Tunis reflects the colour and atmosphere of the present day but still haunted by the ghosts of wartime. Both sea and sky, in incredible shades of blue, are contrasted against white buildings, strong shadows and palm trees. Women in burqas flit around in the shadows and men sit for hours in coffee-shops and teahouses; the souk is full of carpet sellers and small dark shops where craftsmen hammer out brassware or sew leather bags and belts; the butchers' open stalls have cows' heads hooked up along with whole sheep, blood trickling down to the ground. The J.M. Cairns (no relation) comes from the military cemetery at Oued Zarga, which sits in the shade of a blackened and half-demolished colonial church. Two hundred and thirty-nine British and Indian soldiers are buried here overlooking a flooded valley with skeletal dead trees emerging from the water.

Everything in the painting exists now, apart from the ghosts. My father kept the two hens—Black and White (named after the whisky), to provide eggs to augment his limited rations.

The majority of the men, my father included, had never been abroad, so arriving in Algeria and travelling into Tunisia must have been an incredible experience, filled with fear and trepidation. I had only travelled in Europe and North America so I, in part, shared his experience.

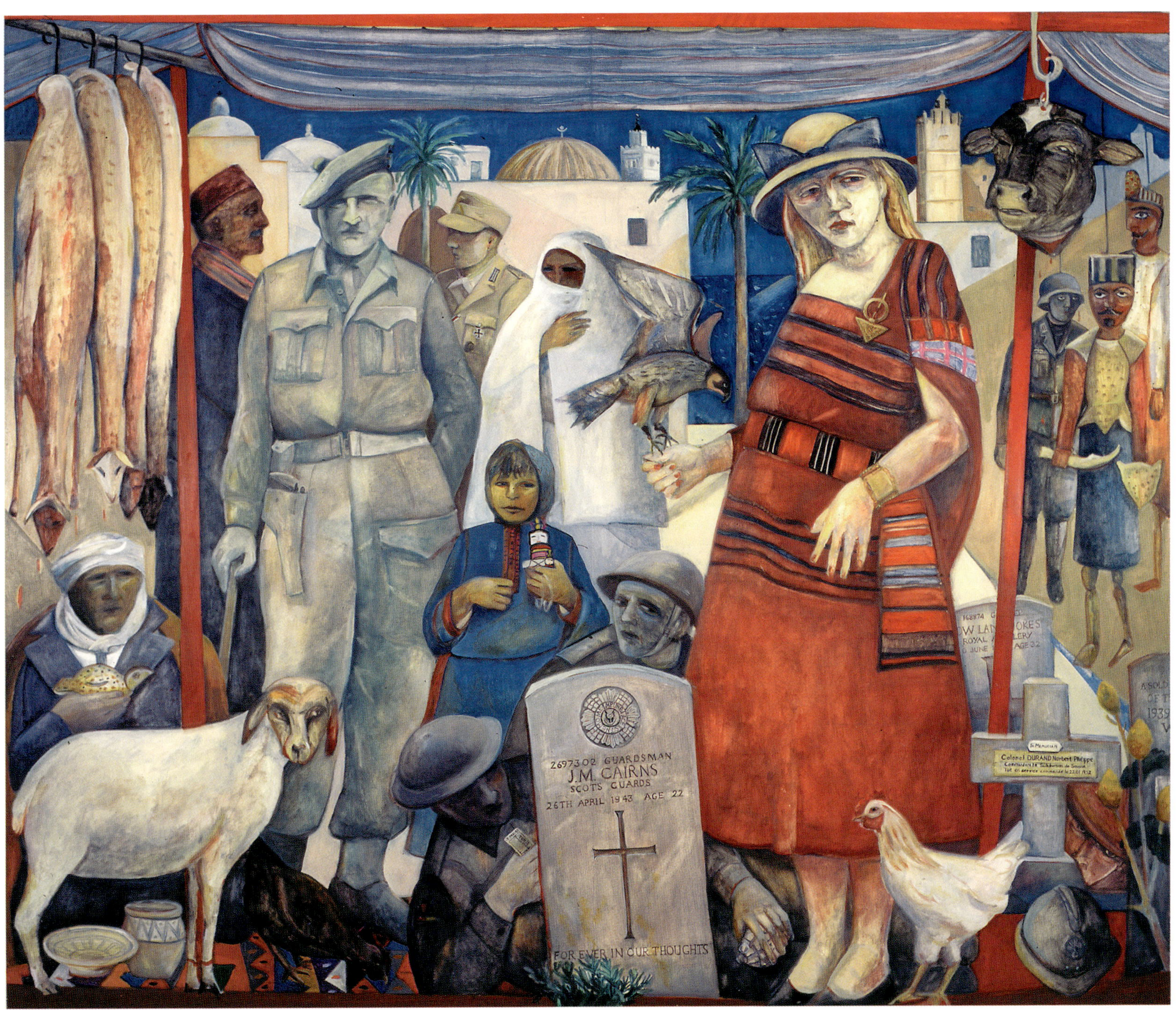
2697302 GUARDSMAN
J.M. CAIRNS
SCOTS GUARDS
26TH APRIL 1943 AGE 22
FOR EVER IN OUR THOUGHTS
Colonel DURAND Norbert Philippe

PLATE FOURTEEN

Longstop Hill, 1995–96

Oil on panels, 213 x 244 cm

This memorial, commemorating the battle for Longstop Hill, is situated at the foot of a tree-covered ridge in the dusty hamlet of El Heri. Arabs sit around while sheep wander aimlessly. This hill was the scene of bitter fighting several times during the campaign and the painting reflects the countryside with its vegetation and the Roman remains at El Dougga. An imaginary tour of the battlefield is taking place with my father riding a particularly bad-tempered camel that I had encountered in El Jem.

The two Arabs at the foot of the memorial looked most suspicious when I stopped to take some photographs and seemed to have time to sit for hours doing very little.

There are apparently still some gun emplacements up in the hills but we did not think it wise to venture up the wooded hillside on our own, as when we had visited a secluded Military Cemetery in Thibar we were followed by a group of Arab youths carrying catapults and just managed to get back to the car as the stones started flying.

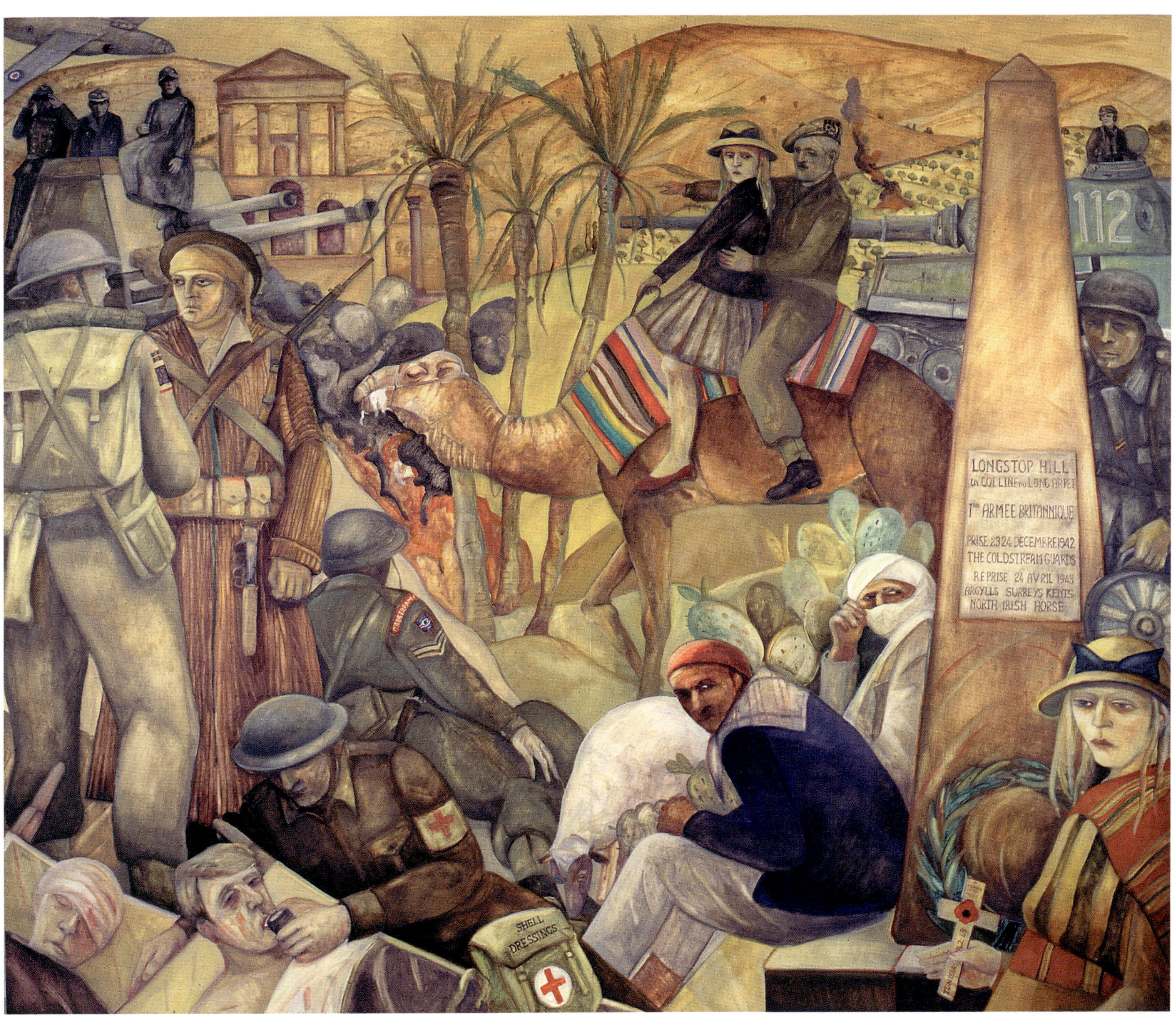
112
LONGSTOP HILL
LA COLLINE DU LONG ARRET
1ère ARMEE BRITANNIQUE
PRISE 23 24 DECEMBRE 1942
THE COLDSTREAM GUARDS
REPRISE 24 AVRIL 1943
ARGYLLS SURREYS KENTS
NORTH IRISH HORSE
SHELL
DRESSINGS

PLATE FIFTEEN

Mothers' Sons, 1996

Oil on panels, 213 x 244 cm

A grim and depressing mausoleum at Cedria Plage, Hamman Lif in Tunisia was built in 1975 to house the eight thousand, five hundred and sixty two soldiers who were exhumed from scattered war graves, and their remains then placed in these communal granite sarcophagi.

This painting is not intended to glorify the German Army but rather to symbolise the waste of young life and empathise with the sorrow felt by all mothers who lose sons in foreign wars. The British in North Africa had respect for Rommel and his Afrika Corps and spoke of many acts of gentlemanly behaviour between the opposing sides.

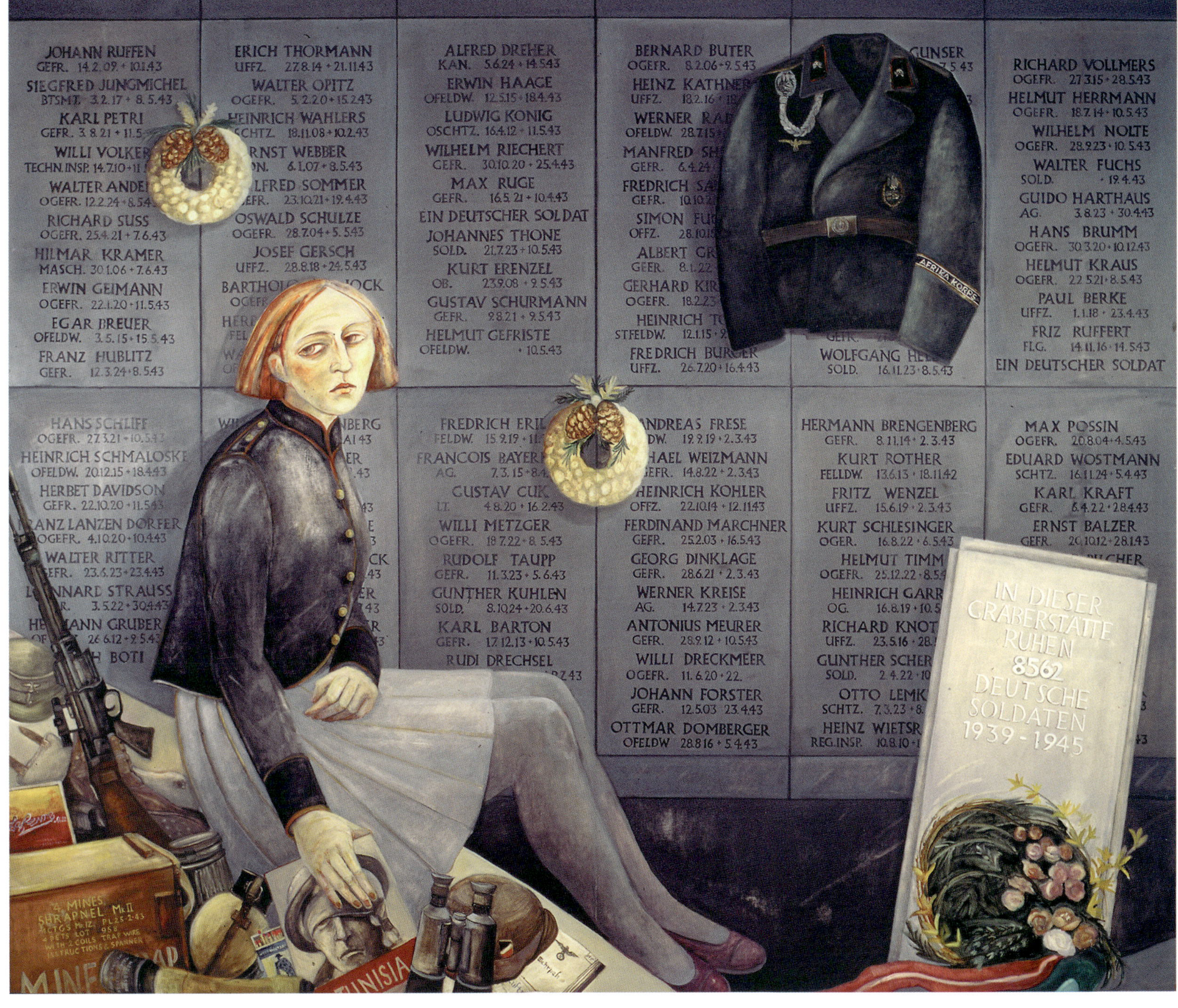
JOHANN RUFFEN
GEFR. 14.2.09 + 10.1.43
SIEGFRED JUNGMICHEL
BTSMT. 3.2.17 + 8.5.43
KARL PETRI
RICHARD SUSS
OGEFR. 25.4.21 + 7.6.43
HILMAR KRAMER
MASCH. 30.1.06 + 7.6.43
ERWIN GEIMANN
OGEFR. 22.1.20 + 11.5.43
EGAR BREUER
OFELDW. 3.5.15 + 15.5.43
FRANZ HUBLITZ
GEFR. 12.3.24 + 8.5.43
ERICH THORMANN
UFFZ. 27.8.14 + 21.11.43
WALTER OPITZ
OGEFR. 5.2.20 + 15.2.43
OSWALD SCHULZE
OGEFR. 28.7.04 + 5.5.43
JOSEF GERSCH
UFFZ. 28.8.18 + 24.5.43
ALFRED DREHER
KAN. 5.6.24 + 14.5.43
ERWIN HAAGE
OFELDW. 12.5.15 + 18.4.43
LUDWIG KONIG
OSCHTZ. 16.4.12 + 11.5.43
WILHELM RIECHERT
GEFR. 30.10.20 + 25.4.43
MAX RUGE
GEFR. 16.5.21 + 10.4.43
EIN DEUTSCHER SOLDAT
JOHANNES THONE
SOLD. 21.7.23 + 10.5.43
KURT ERENZEL
OB. 23.9.08 + 9.5.43
GUSTAV SCHURMANN
GEFR. 9.8.21 + 9.5.43
HELMUT GEFRISTE
OFELDW. + 10.5.43
BERNARD BUTER
OGEFR. 8.2.06 + 9.5.43
FREDRICH BURGER
UFFZ. 26.7.20 + 16.4.43
AFRIKA KORPS
RICHARD VOLLMERS
OGEFR. 27.3.15 + 28.5.43
HELMUT HERRMANN
OGEFR. 18.7.14 + 10.5.43
WILHELM NOLTE
OGEFR. 28.9.23 + 10.5.43
WALTER FUCHS
SOLD. + 19.4.43
GUIDO HARTHAUS
AG. 3.8.23 + 30.4.43
HANS BRUMM
OGEFR. 30.3.20 + 10.12.43
HELMUT KRAUS
OGEFR. 22.5.21 + 8.5.43
PAUL BERKE
UFFZ. 1.1.18 + 23.4.43
FRIZ RUFFERT
FLG. 14.11.16 + 14.5.43
EIN DEUTSCHER SOLDAT
HANS SCHLIFF
OGEFR. 27.3.21 + 10.5.43
HEINRICH SCHMALOSKE
OFELDW. 20.12.15 + 18.4.43
HERBET DAVIDSON
GEFR. 22.10.20 + 11.5.43
WILLI METZGER
OGEFR. 18.7.22 + 8.5.43
RUDOLF TAUPP
GEFR. 11.3.23 + 5.6.43
GUNTHER KUHLEN
SOLD. 8.10.24 + 20.6.43
KARL BARTON
GEFR. 17.12.13 + 10.5.43
RUDI DRECHSEL
HEINRICH KOHLER
OFFZ. 22.10.14 + 12.11.43
FERDINAND MARCHNER
GEFR. 25.2.03 + 16.5.43
GEORG DINKLAGE
GEFR. 28.6.21 + 2.3.43
WERNER KREISE
AG. 14.7.23 + 2.3.43
ANTONIUS MEURER
GEFR. 28.9.12 + 10.5.43
WILLI DRECKMEER
JOHANN FORSTER
GEFR. 12.5.03 23.4.43
OTTMAR DOMBERGER
OFELDW 28.8.16 + 5.4.43
HERMANN BRENGENBERG
GEFR. 8.11.14 + 2.3.43
KURT ROTHER
FELLDW. 13.6.13 + 18.11.42
FRITZ WENZEL
UFFZ. 15.6.19 + 2.3.43
KURT SCHLESINGER
OGER. 16.8.22 + 6.5.43
MAX POSSIN
OGEFR. 20.8.04 + 4.5.43
EDUARD WOSTMANN
SCHTZ. 16.11.24 + 5.4.43
KARL KRAFT
GEFR. 8.4.22 + 28.4.43
ERNST BALZER
IN DIESER GRABERSTÄTTE RUHEN 8562 DEUTSCHE SOLDATEN 1939 - 1945
4 MINES SHRAPNEL Mk II
TUNISIA

PLATE SIXTEEN

Sword Beach, 1996

Oil on panels, 213 × 366 cm

It was cold and snowing when we were in Normandy, making the terrain and the military cemeteries bleak and clear and the bocage seem less dense. Some of the smaller museums were closed but those in Caen and Arromanche provided excellent source material. At Pegasus Bridge, where gliders landed and near the Café Gondree, gun emplacements are still evident and armoured vehicles and tanks sit as if waiting for their drivers and crews to return.

When I planned this work, I was under the impression that my father had landed on D–Day, along with the 3rd Infantry, but I have since found out that he landed later. Curiously enough, I did not paint him as one of the combatants but he features on the locket around my neck. Having walked along the beaches and viewed the memorials, I had to paint something that commemorated that momentous day.

Bill Millin features in the right hand corner, painted as he was in 1996 rather than at the age when he piped Lord Lovat's Commandos off the landing craft and on to the beach.

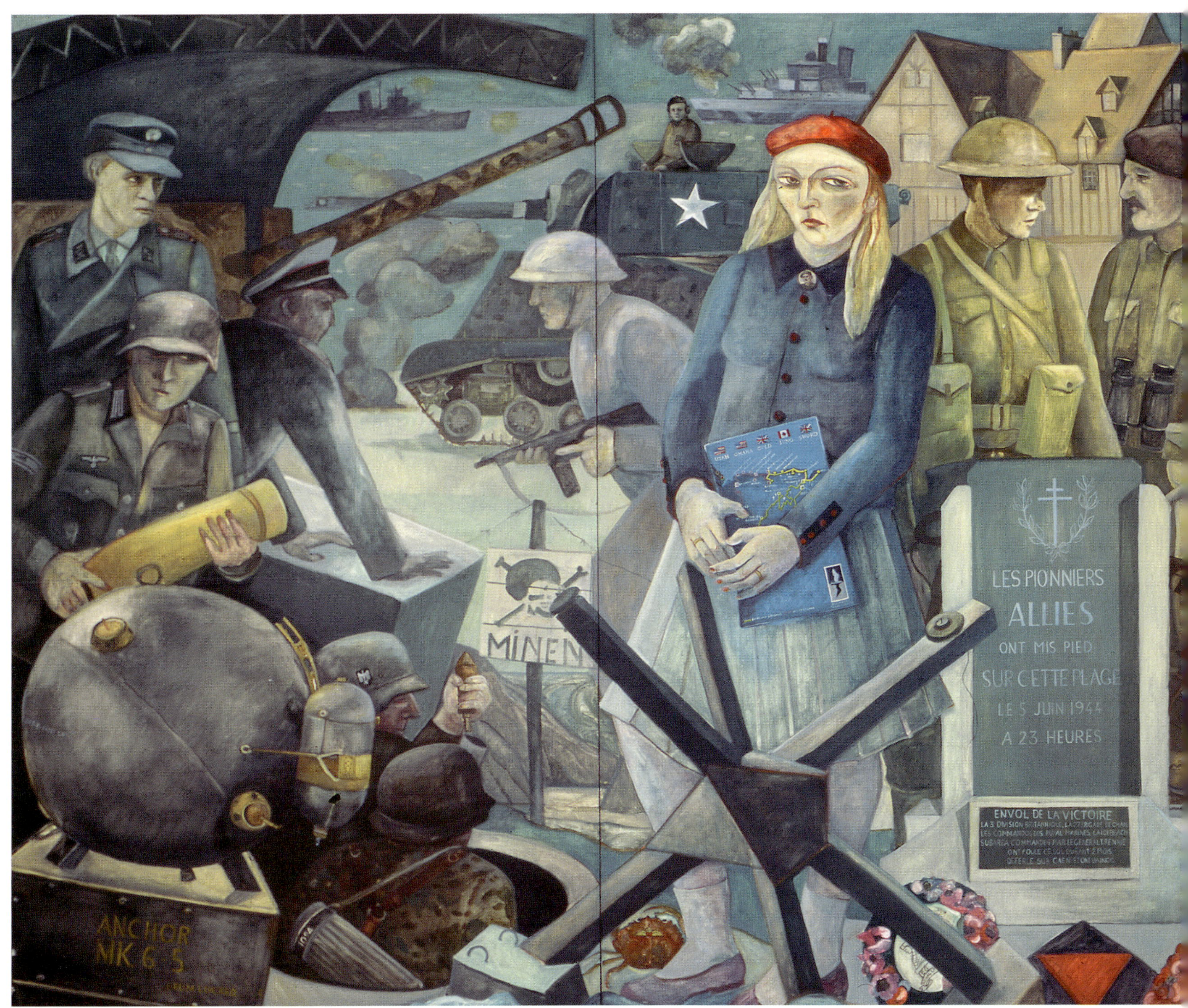
UTAH
OMAHA
MINEN
LES PIONNIERS
ALLIES
ONT MIS PIED
SUR CETTE PLAGE
LE 5 JUIN 1944
A 23 HEURES
ENVOL DE LA VICTOIRE
ANCHOR
MK 6 5

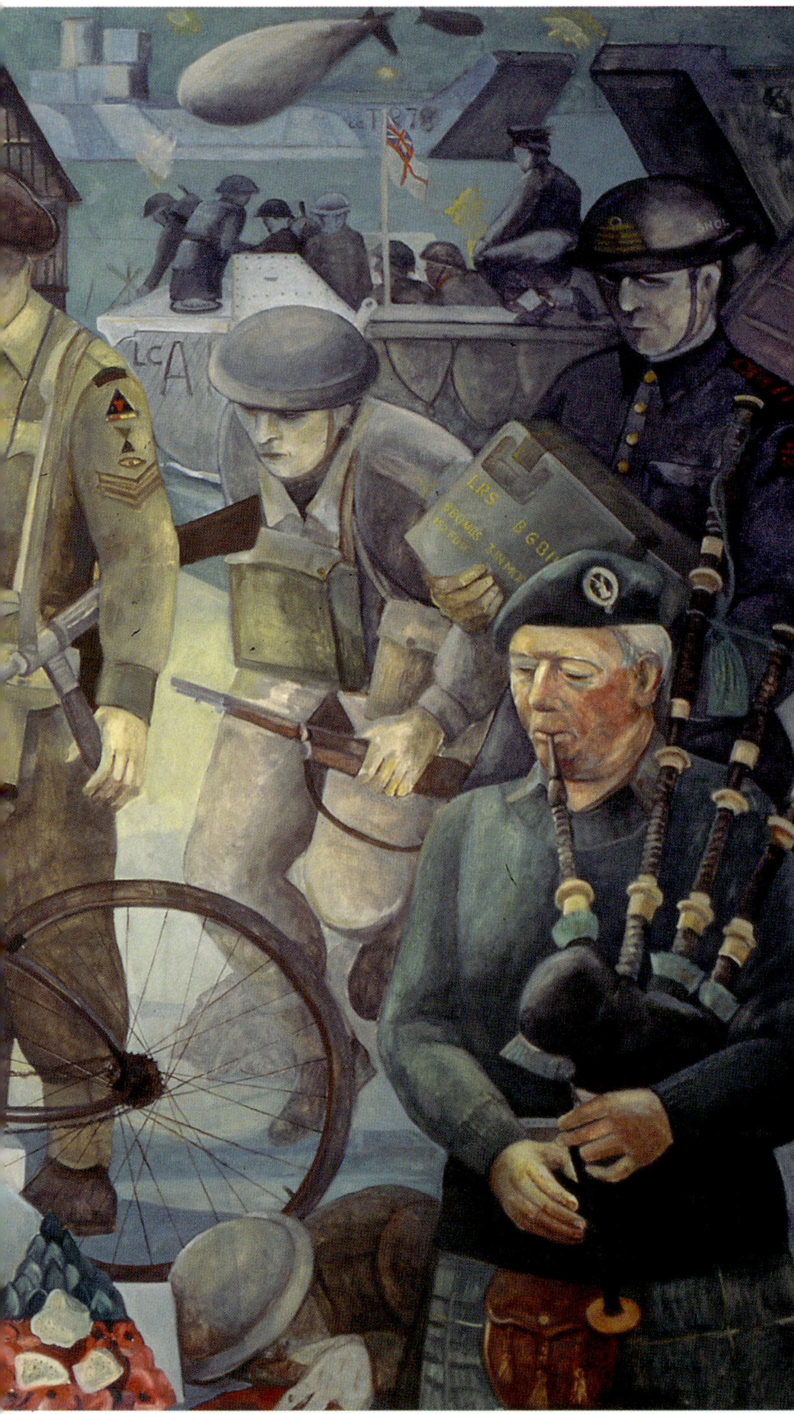

Gravestones are set in the winter landscape, many for soldiers who died on June 6, 1944. Those shown here were taken from the Ranville and Bayeux Military Cemeteries.

This painting started from a photograph of my father with a dog and is inscribed on the reverse: 'A soldier and his friend'. While in Normandy he found an injured Alsatian which was to be put down, but she looked at him so appealingly that he took her to the army surgeon who sewed her up. He called the dog Villette, supposedly after the place he had found her. On our trip to Normandy in February 1996, we found this small hamlet high on a wooded ridge overlooking the valley; a natural vantage point and an obvious location for a camp. The dog was taught to sniff out Germans and was with Dad all the way to Bremen.

All the family feature in this work, including, lying in the snow, a photograph of my mother. My elder brother and two sisters are painted as they were when father went to war. My younger brother and I were born after the war. He is holding the ambulance toy and I am the nine year old schoolgirl, holding a hen, one of war's victims.

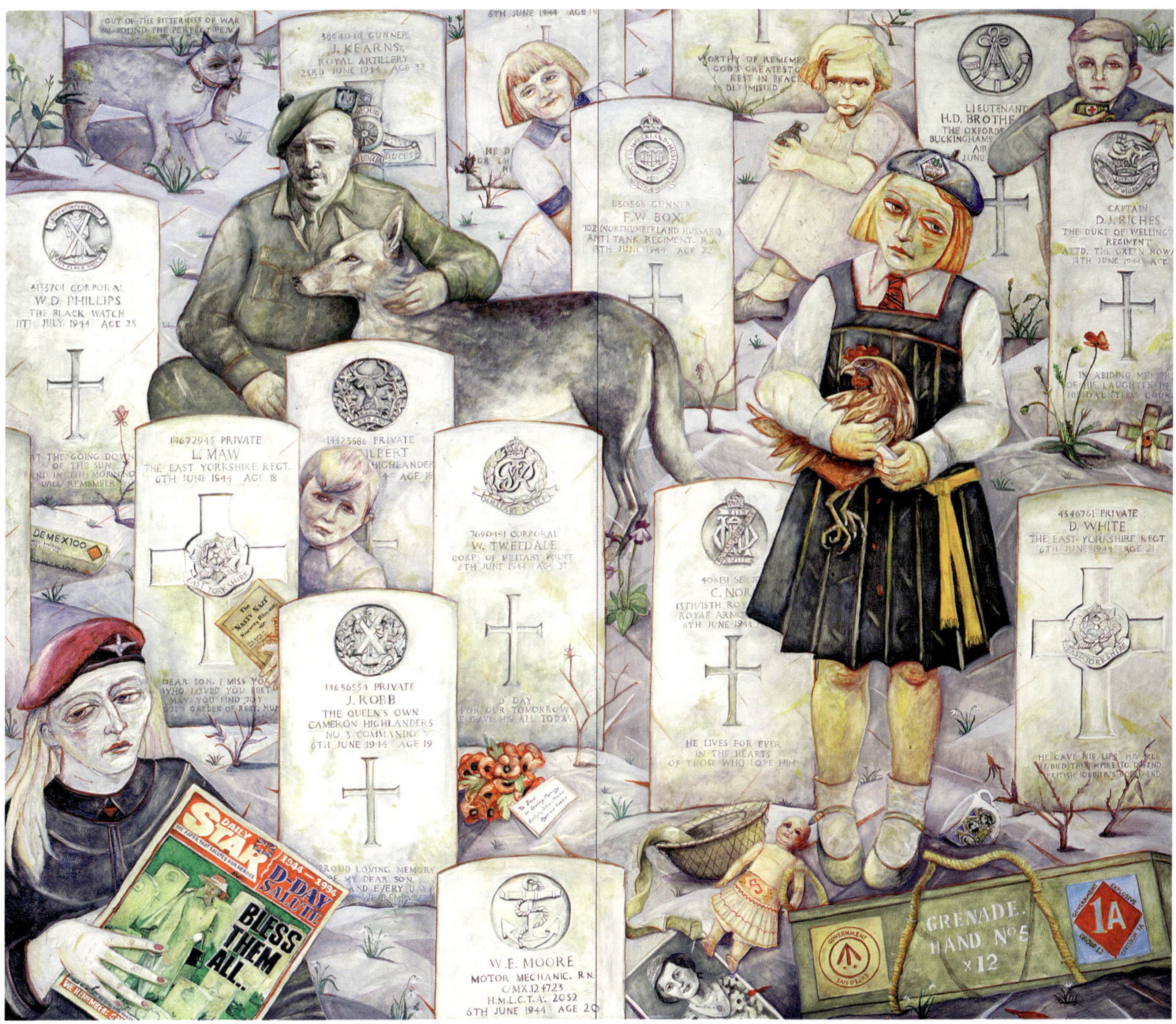

OUT OF THE BITTERNESS OF WAR
HE FOUND THE PERFECT PEACE
3864049 GUNNER
J. KEARNS
ROYAL ARTILLERY
23RD JUNE 1944 AGE 32
LIEUTENANT
3133701 CORPORAL
W.D. PHILLIPS
THE BLACK WATCH
11TH JULY 1944 AGE 28
1130568 GUNNER
F.W. BOX
102 (NORTHUMBERLAND HUSSARS)
ANTI TANK REGIMENT. R.A.
13TH JUNE 1944 AGE 22
CAPTAIN
D.J. RICHES
14672945 PRIVATE
L. MAW
THE EAST YORKSHIRE REGT.
6TH JUNE 1944 AGE 18
EAST YORKSHIRE
14423586 PRIVATE
DEMEX100
7690191 CORPORAL
W. TWEEDALE
CORPS OF MILITARY POLICE
6TH JUNE 1944 AGE 37
4546761 PRIVATE
D. WHITE
THE EAST YORKSHIRE REGT.
6TH JUNE 1944 AGE 21
14656554 PRIVATE
J. ROBB
THE QUEEN'S OWN
CAMERON HIGHLANDERS
NO. 3 COMMANDO
6TH JUNE 1944 AGE 19
D DAY
HE LIVES FOR EVER
IN THE HEARTS
OF THOSE WHO LOVE HIM
W.E. MOORE
MOTOR MECHANIC. R.N.
C/MX.124723
H.M.L.C.T.A. 2052
6TH JUNE 1944 AGE 20
DAILY STAR
1944–1994
D-DAY SALUTE
BLESS THEM ALL..
GRENADE.
HAND No 5
x12
1A

PLATE EIGHTEEN

War Tourist, 1998

Oil on panel, 183 x 122 cm

This work was a summary of the project at a point where I wanted to stress my own physical involvement by depicting myself in the act of painting; a portrait of my father and myself. I am in Berber costume with sun hat and camera, as the war tourist. The table in the foreground displays a selection of my father's memorabilia and a basket of wooden birds which I bought in Cracow.

There is a fragment from *After the Battle* and in the background, the Canada Memorial at Vancouver Corner, near Passchendaele. The column marks the battlefield where eighteen thousand Canadians withstood the first German gas attacks in April 1915. Two thousand died and are buried nearby.

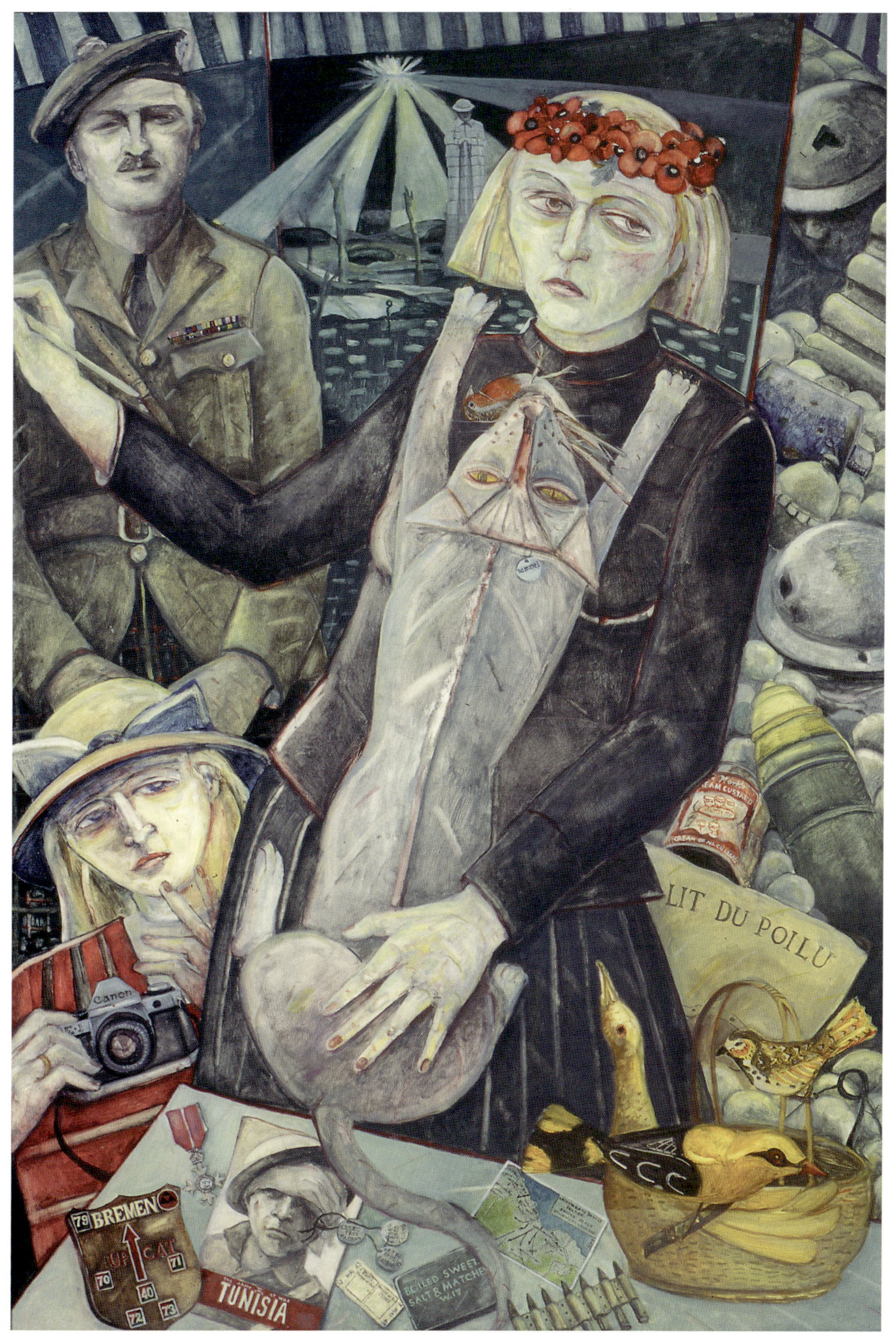

LIT DU POILU
Canon
BREMEN
TUNISIA
BOILED SWEETS
SALT & MATCHES

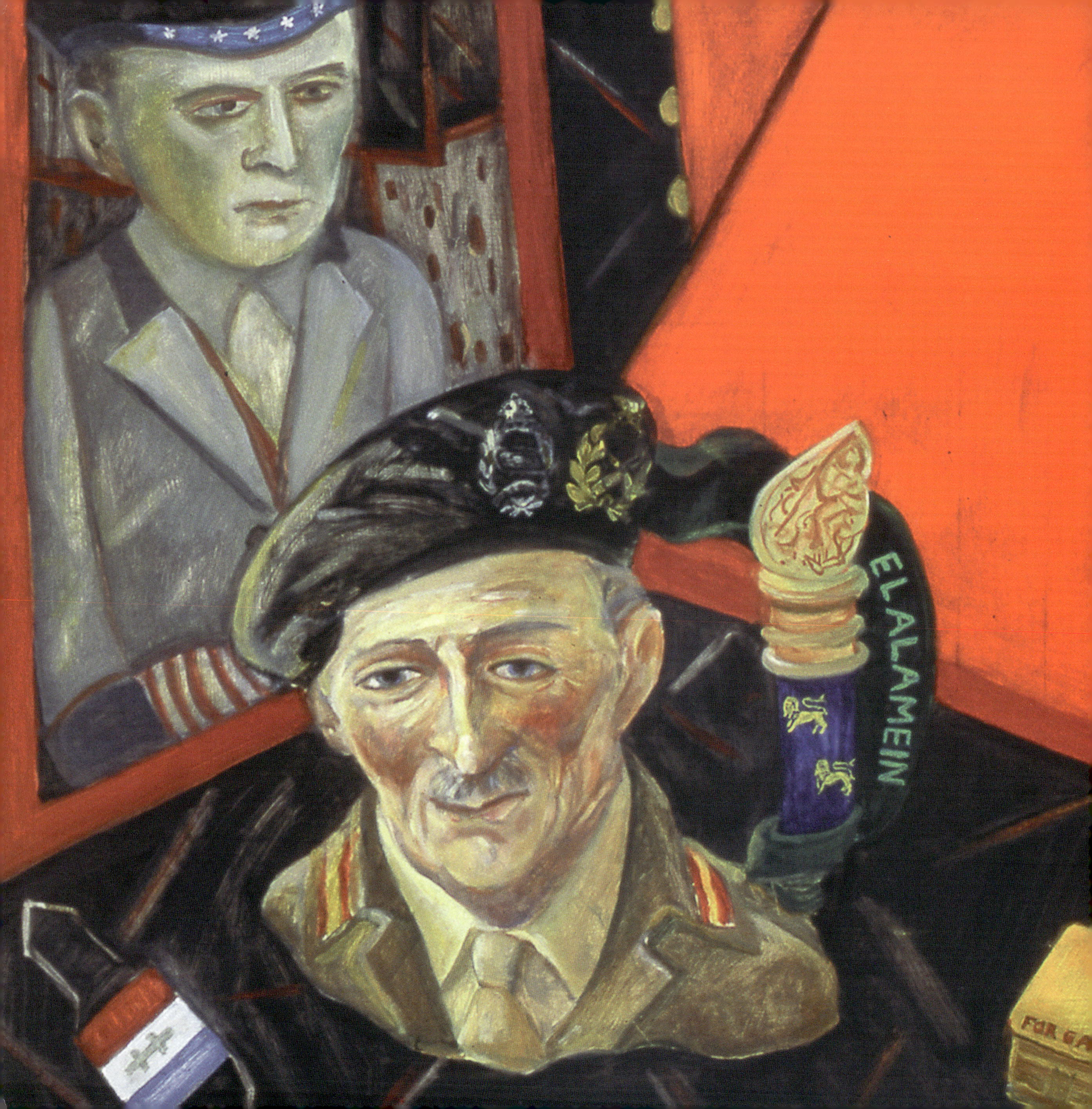
ELALAMEIN

THE HOME FRONT

When I was a young student I used to scour the thrift shops of Aberdeen looking for second-hand clothes from the late thirties and forties. I felt at home in these outfits and used to wonder what their previous owners were like. In my first year at art school I had a landlady who had lived in the Lake District during the war. She had many stories about the American soldiers stationed in the area and told me that in the mornings after a dance the surrounding trees would be decorated with condoms.

I remember my late aunts describing how, in wartime, they used to paint their legs with gravy browning and then draw a line up the back of each leg to simulate stockings. Life on the home front was all about make-do and mend, and the government issued many leaflets ranging from *Home defence* to *What to do in a gas attack*, from *Digging for victory with Potato Pete's recipe book*, to *How to look after your pets in wartime*. I see these leaflets in war museums and never fail to be fascinated.

I remember as a child the rows of metal stumps along low walls where the ornamental railings had been removed to be reprocessed into ships and tanks. Aluminium pots and pans were also taken to provide lightweight metal for aircraft. During the blackout householders had to ensure that no light could be seen through their windows and special blackout material was available for curtains which we children used after the war for dressing up. Air Raid Prevention wardens patrolled the streets after dark ensuring that no chinks of light could attract the enemy bombers. In the painting, *Messerschmitt over Footdee* I am the ARP warden not the naked temptress.

PLATE NINETEEN

The Anderson Shelter, 2004

Oil on panel, 183 × 122 cm

COURTESY OF
ABERDEEN ASSET MANAGEMENT PLC

During the war many families were provided with Anderson shelters made from curved sheets of corrugated steel. They were constructed over a trench dug in the garden and earth was then shovelled back over the structure to give added protection and extra growing space for vegetables. When the air raid sirens sounded, one was meant to go to the shelter for protection until the raid was over. They were pretty basic—damp, cold and uncomfortable and would certainly not have stood a direct hit.

I have shown my mother and the pre-war family in the shelter but relocated to Footdee, where I now live. My younger brother and I are outside looking in, as we had not been born at this time. On the table is a selection of goods intermittently available during wartime, along with a cup and saucer from the family tea set. Fish was unrationed but the single pork chop was half the weekly meat ration. Although shown in the painting, our cat, Kipper, was not around until the early fifties but she was taken into the countryside and abandoned after she stole the fish intended for supper, leaving me broken-hearted.

My eldest sister was always passionately interested in clothes and she is shown at the bottom of the painting studying 'Economy Frocks', a magazine full of dress patterns. During the war and into the fifties many people had to make their own clothes using anything from blankets to old curtains, as fabric too was rationed.

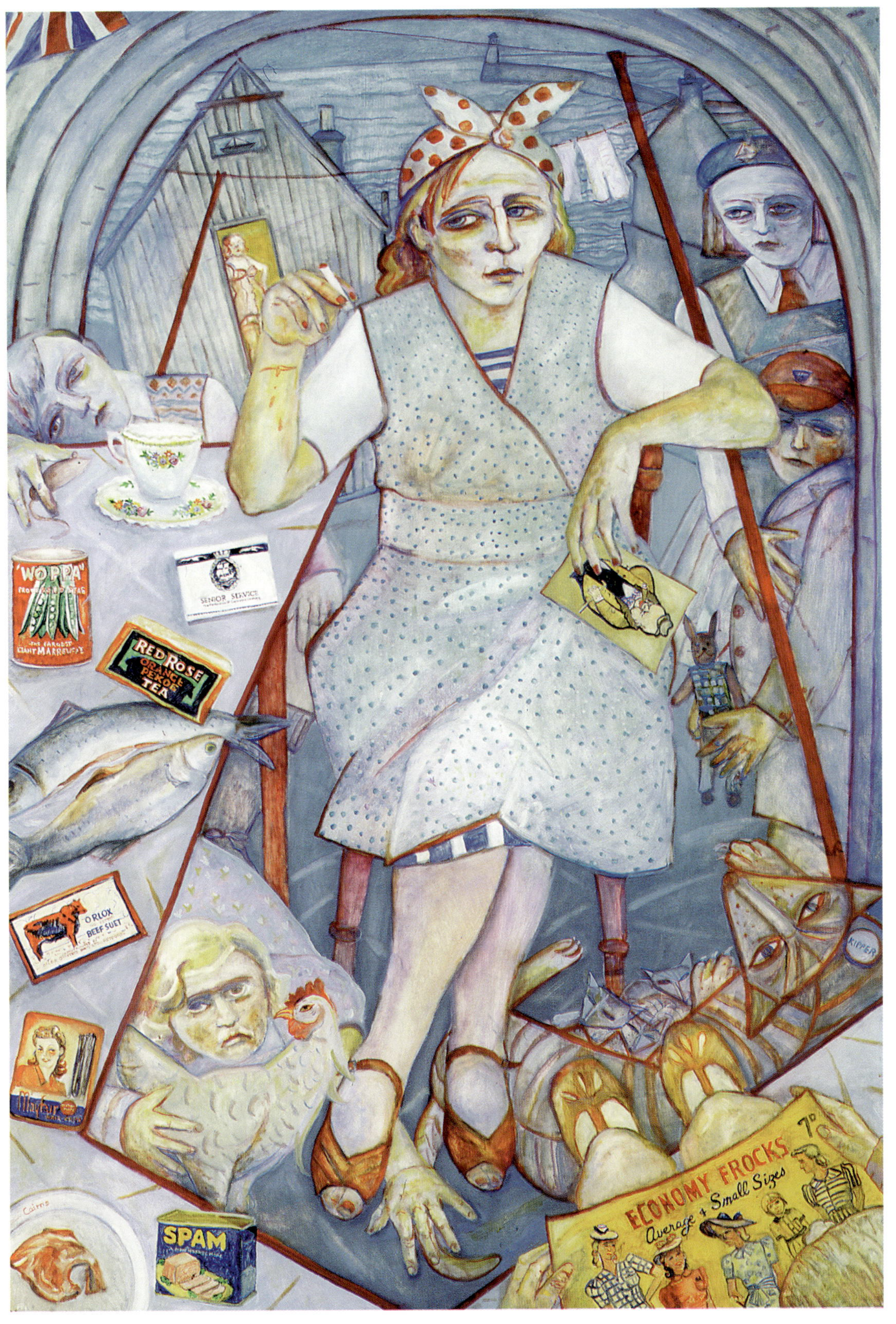
SENIOR SERVICE
RED ROSE
ORANGE PEKOE TEA
ORLOX
BEEF SUET
SPAM
KIPPER
ECONOMY FROCKS
Average + Small Sizes
7D

PLATE TWENTY

Messerschmitt over Footdee, 2003

Oil on panel, 152 × 122 cm

Hall Russell's, the shipyard in Footdee, and the Neptune Bar opposite, were bombed in 1940; I believe by a Heinkel but, for the painting, I used a Messerschmitt based on a construction kit I had been given for my fiftieth birthday. Thirty-two shipyard workers were killed and a hundred were injured. From my window in Footdee I could have seen the searchlights and the bomber coming in over the sea with the ack-ack guns of the Torry Battery aiming to shoot it down.

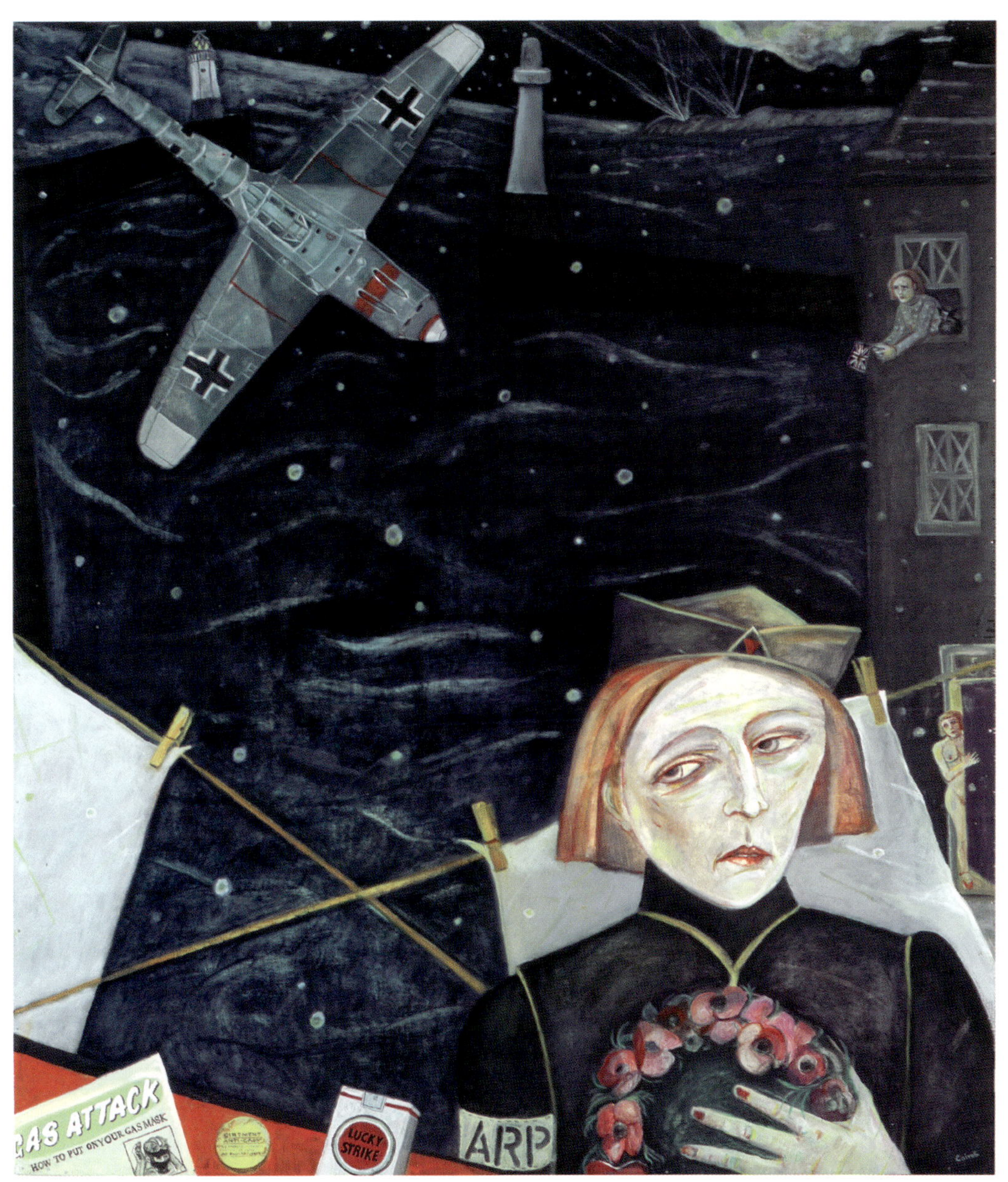
GAS ATTACK
HOW TO PUT ON YOUR GAS MASK
OINTMENT ANTI-GAS
LUCKY STRIKE
ARP

PLATE TWENTY–ONE

Bonjour Field Marshall, 2002

Oil on panel, 183 x 122 cm

This painting is a tribute to Field Marshall Sir Bernard Montgomery for whom my father had tremendous respect and admiration. During the war the less appealing side of his character was not apparent to the majority of his officers or men and he was seen as a formidable operational commander who brought victory in Egypt after a depressing period with few successes.

My 'Monty' Toby jug is on the table along with two others from museum collections and on one side of the mirrored family dressing table is an angel of death and opposite, a schoolgirl clutching a hen, again the victim. In the painting I am wearing a frock which reminded me of British military dress uniform, offering an invitation to 'Monty' to celebrate his victories over a can of milk.

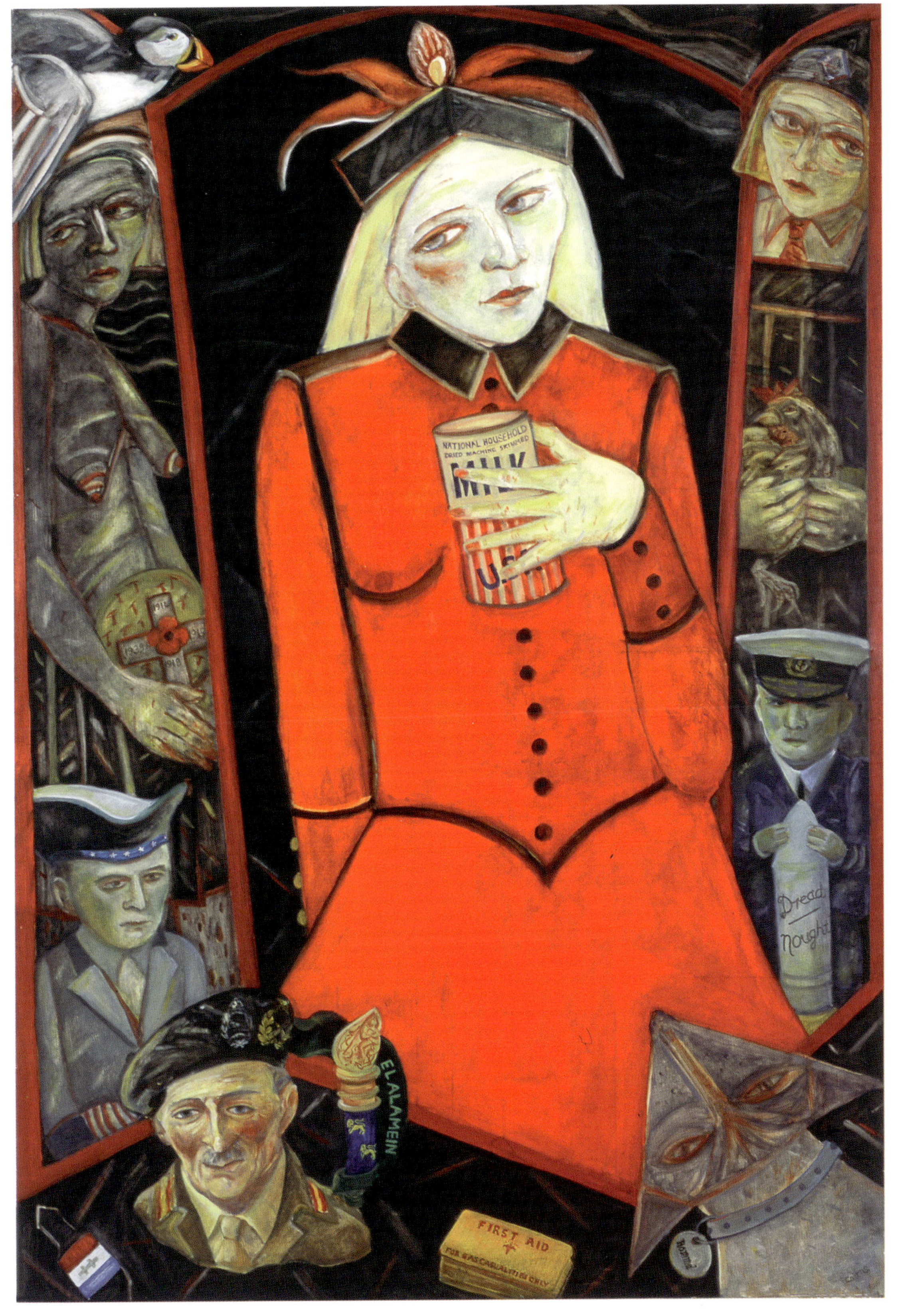
NATIONAL HOUSEHOLD
DRIED MACHINE SKIMMED
Dread
nought
EL ALAMEIN
FIRST AID
FOR GAS CASUALTIES ONLY

PLATE TWENTY–TWO

Pusser's Rum, 2002
Oil on panel, 122 x 91 cm

In the D–Day Museum in Portsmouth I found the leaflet: *How to look after your pets in wartime*. City dwellers were encouraged to either evacuate their animals or have them put down and in the first days of the war some four hundred thousand London pets were humanely gassed by the RSPCA. Dogs were not allowed in public shelters, nor was it recommended that they share family shelters in case they panicked when bombs fell. Cats, on the other hand, were less of a problem while caged birds and goldfish went to and from the shelters with their owners.

In the corner of the painting is my cat Rommel, so called because of his field grey coat and propensity for spending much of his time out on manoeuvres.

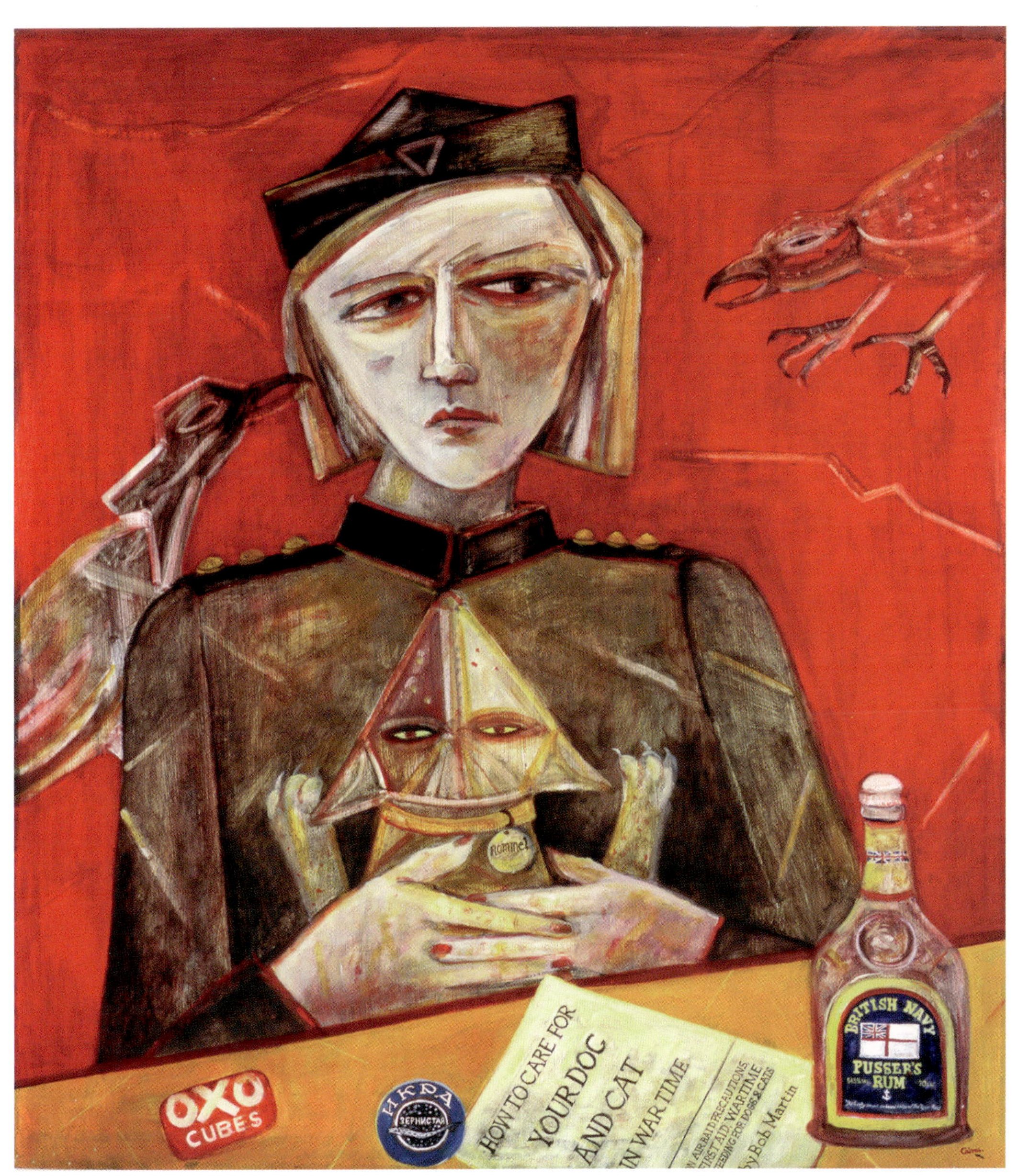

Rommel
OXO
CUBES
ИКРА
ЗЕРНИСТАЯ
HOW TO CARE FOR
YOUR DOG
AND CAT
IN WARTIME
By Bob Martin
BRITISH NAVY
PUSSER'S
RUM

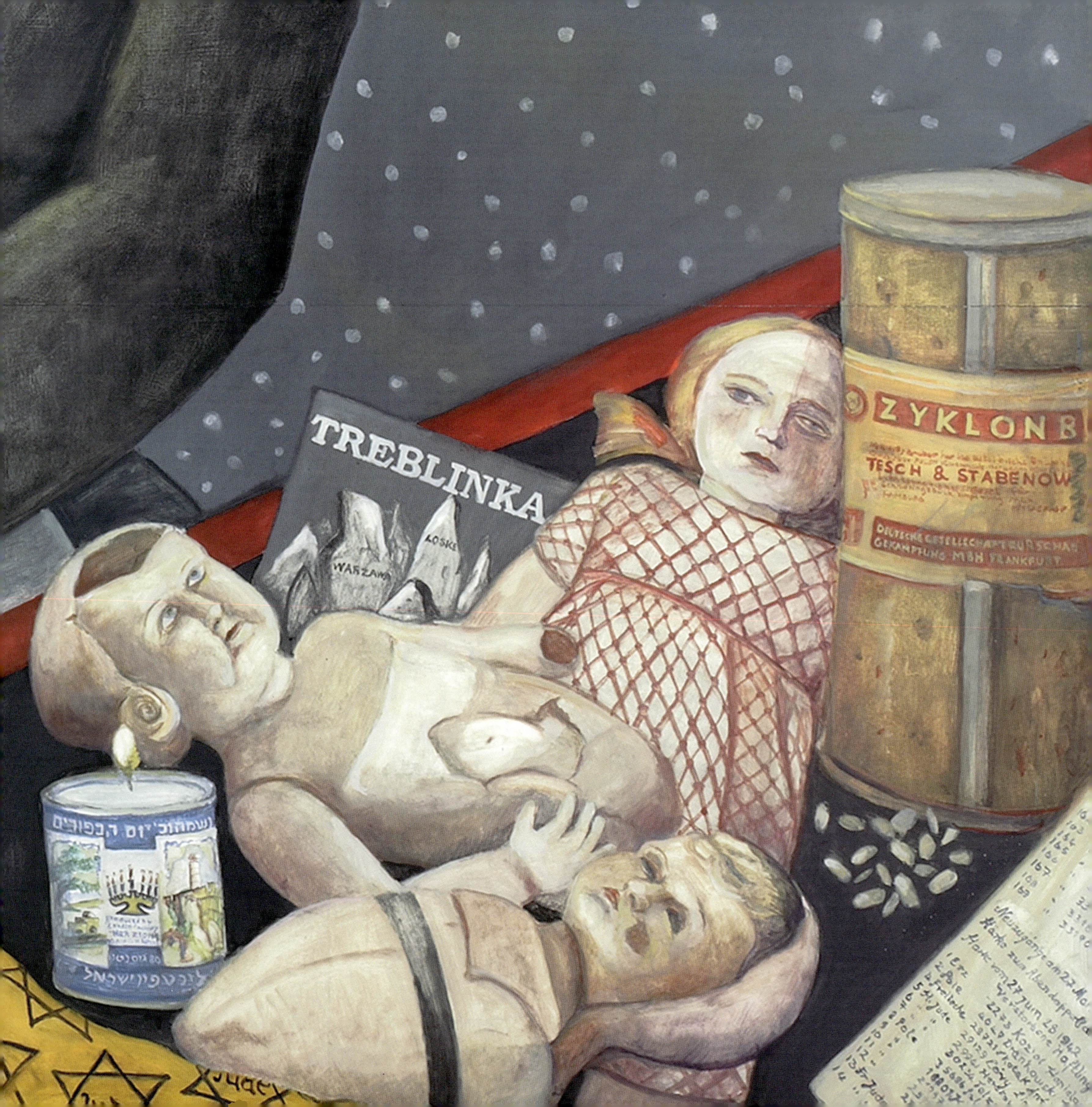
TREBLINKA
WARZAWA
ZYKLON B
TESCH & STABENOW

GERMANY AND POLAND

In 1995 I arranged to go with Milestone on their 'Third Reich Tour'. I thought that it would give me a more direct experience and greater understanding of the people, places and events about which I had only read. After visiting the Wannsee Centre in Berlin, Dachau and Mauthausen concentration camps, Terezin, and Lidice, I felt it necessary to continue my journey on to Poland.

It was never my intention to create paintings depicting the Holocaust. I felt that I had no right, nor could I even begin to portray the suffering, torture, barbarity and genocide which the Nazis inflicted, not only on Jewish people, but also on Russian prisoners of war, gypsies, homosexuals, political prisoners and the populations of countries which they had invaded. In Poland I went to Treblinka, Madjanek, Auschwitz, Birkenau, Gross Rosen and Pawiak Prison in Warsaw, as well as the remains of the Ghettos and Gestapo headquarters.

Nothing could prepare one for the inherent evil and chill of these places where millions had died in unspeakable cruelty and degradation at the hands of the sadists and psychopaths who were part of the German Reich. If selected for the work force, an individual's life expectancy might only be a few months, as in addition to those sent to the gas chambers, many were shot or hanged for minor infractions while others died of dysentery, typhus or malnutrition. Even when it was obvious that the war was lost, the Nazis did not end their reign of terror but forced prisoners on death marches or onto trains without provisions to be sent on interminable journeys causing needless anguish and loss of life.

Again it was the sad belongings, which made me feel, that through them, I could perhaps make a contribution to the remembrance of their owners.

PLATE TWENTY–THREE

Dark Shadows, 1996–97

Oil on panels, 183 x 244 cm

This was my first response to the 'Third Reich Tour'. The background colour and the post with the searchlight came from Dachau; the upturned triangle can be seen as a mound filled with the ashes of victims, while the shell cases, containing their deadly shrapnel, could also be read as coffins. The two girls are adolescent victims, one Russian and one Jewish, one wearing the locket with my father's portrait which features regularly in my paintings. I keep a photograph of my father taken in Tunisia inside my passport so that wherever I go, he comes too. It is my way of involving him, not only as a companion, but also as a witness in these other theatres of war.

The use of planes is symbolic: aggression from the Messerschmitt and retribution from the Spitfire and American Lockheed P38. These came from models similar to those which boys made during the war to help them identify Allied and Axis aircraft. Here too are American ration packs and a British ration card; the fragment of prison uniform is from Dachau, the beer mat advertising that a hotel in Frankfurt was 'Juden Frei', comes from the museum at The Olympic Stadium in Berlin, while the shoe and the shop sign are from Lidice.

In this painting and in *Polish Journey* I have used a bale of yellow cloth covered in black outlined stars, with the word 'Jude' printed in their centres; these stars were ready to be cut out and sewn on to the clothing of Jews. To see this cloth in the Wannsee Centre in Berlin, as if on sale in a fabric shop, really shocked me, bringing home the scale and scope of the German war machine which made ordinary working people party to Nazi genocide.

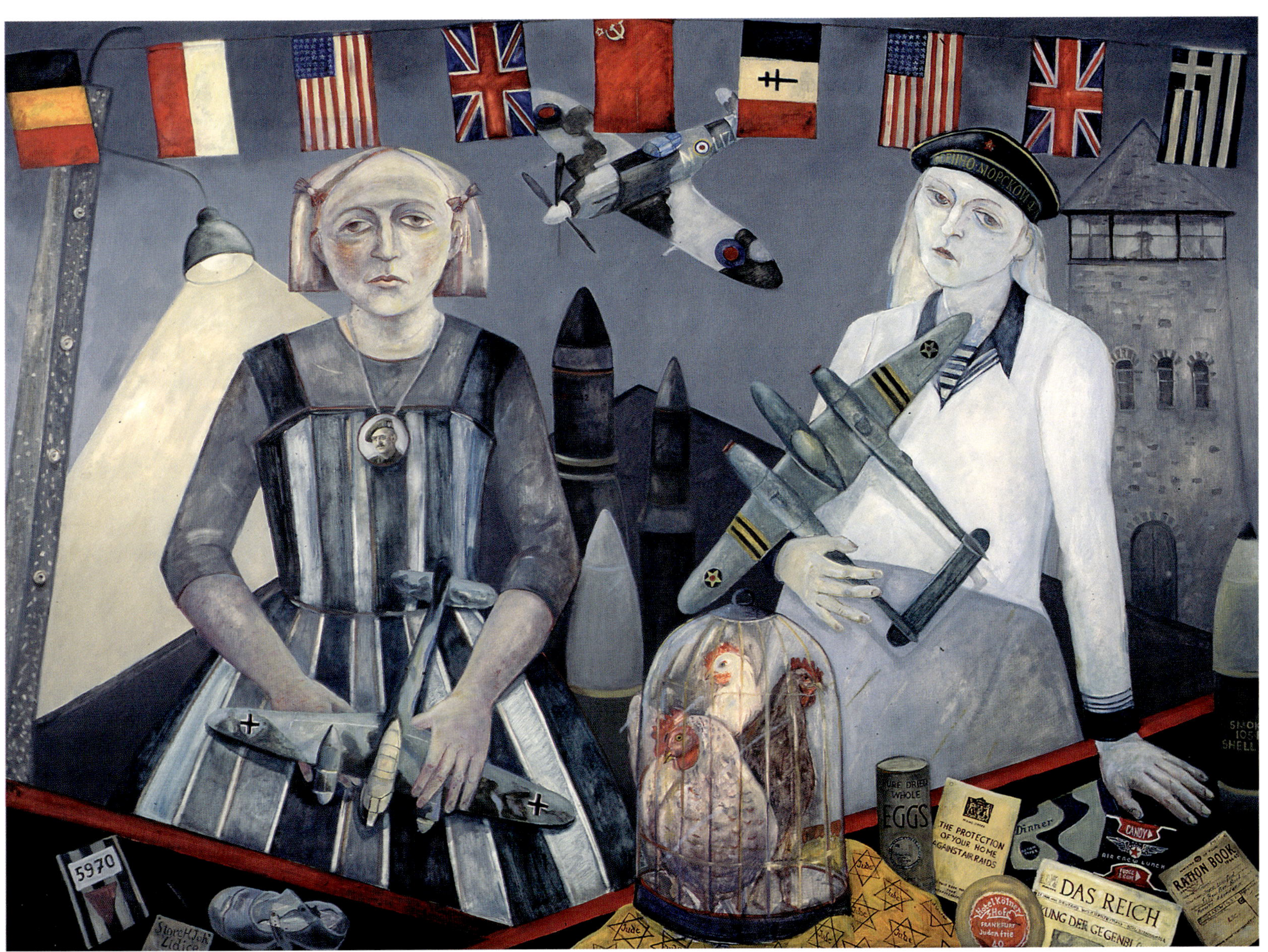

5970
Lidice
WHOLE
EGGS
THE PROTECTION OF YOUR HOME AGAINST AIR RAIDS
Dinner
CANDY
AIR CREW LUNCH
DAS REICH
RATION BOOK
Hotel Kölner Hof
FRANKFURT
Juden frie
Jude

PLATE TWENTY–FOUR

Shoes from Majdanek, 2002–2005

Oil on panels, 183 × 244 cm

Here, in this dreadful and a frightening place, were two huts filled with shoes of all shapes and sizes from baby shoes upwards—approximately eight hundred and twenty thousand pairs. These shoes had come from all over Europe, from Paris, Vienna, Brussels and Warsaw, from Trieste, Prague, Antwerp, Amsterdam and Kiev. The smell of decaying rubber on a warm day was overpowering and the impression was of a dusty grey tortured mass, within which was only an occasional glimpse of colour. There was also a vast circular memorial covering an open urn of equal size, full of ashes amongst which can be discerned recognisable fragments of bone.

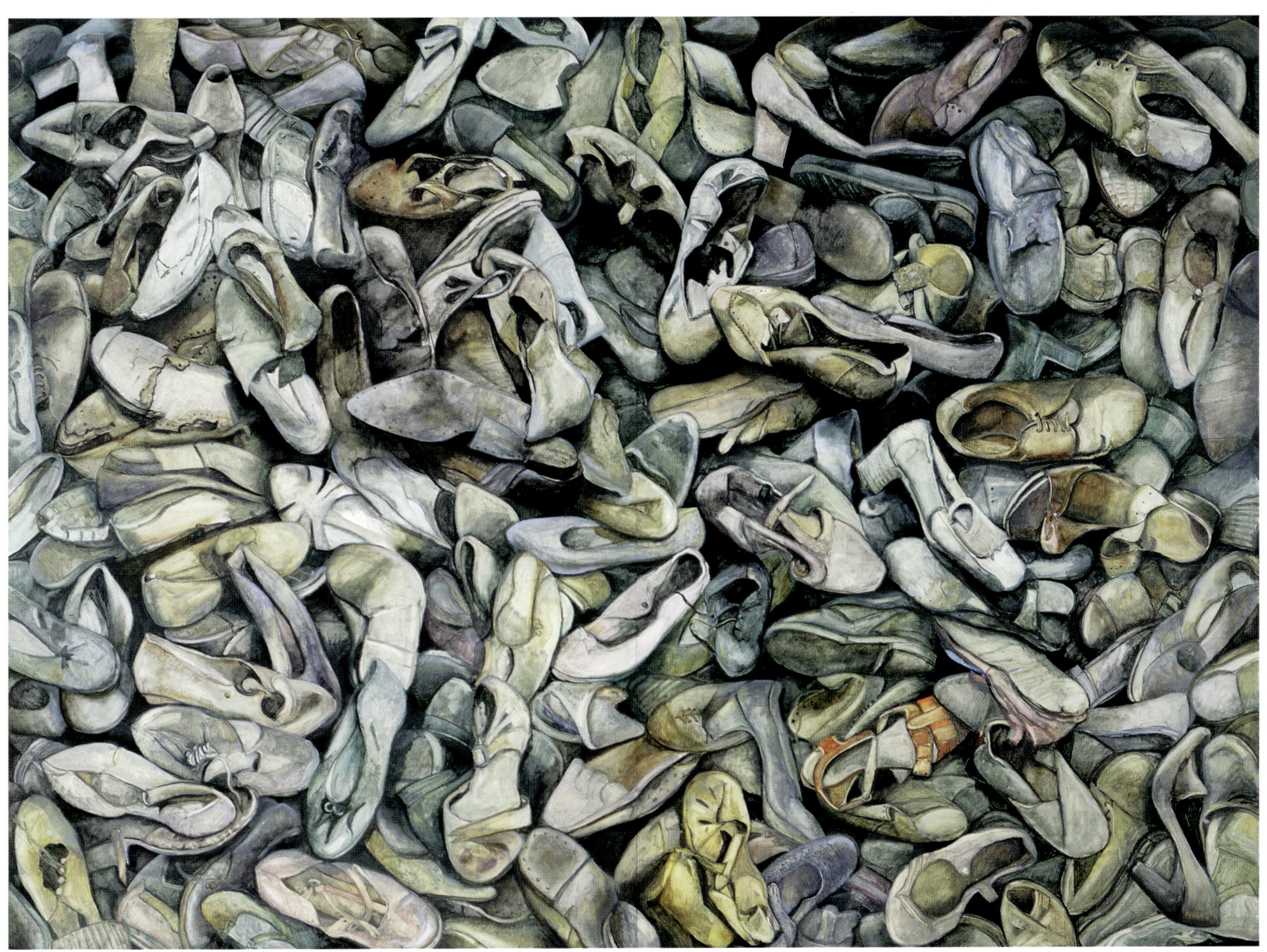

PLATE TWENTY–FIVE

Polish Journey, 1998

Oil on panel, 183 x 183 cm

ROYAL SCOTTISH ACADEMY (DIPLOMA COLLECTION)

Photograph © Antonia Reeve

The main figure wears the father locket and holds a poppy wreath in memory of the murdered children of Treblinka, Terezín, Auschwitz and particularly Madjanek, where there was an area of the camp specifically for children. The dolls come mainly from Madjanek, along with the tin of Zyclone B crystals, used to gas the prisoners. The doll with the suitcase was in the museum at Terezín and the address on the case was taken from one of many piled up in Auschwitz.

Brightly coloured tins containing lit candles are at every memorial site. A member of our tour insisted that I should have one that he had found abandoned in a ditch. Although I did not feel comfortable about this I hope that the refiguration of the candle through my painting may allow it to burn for eternity. Little piles of rocks are left on top of Jewish gravestones and in the crematoria as a mark of respect.

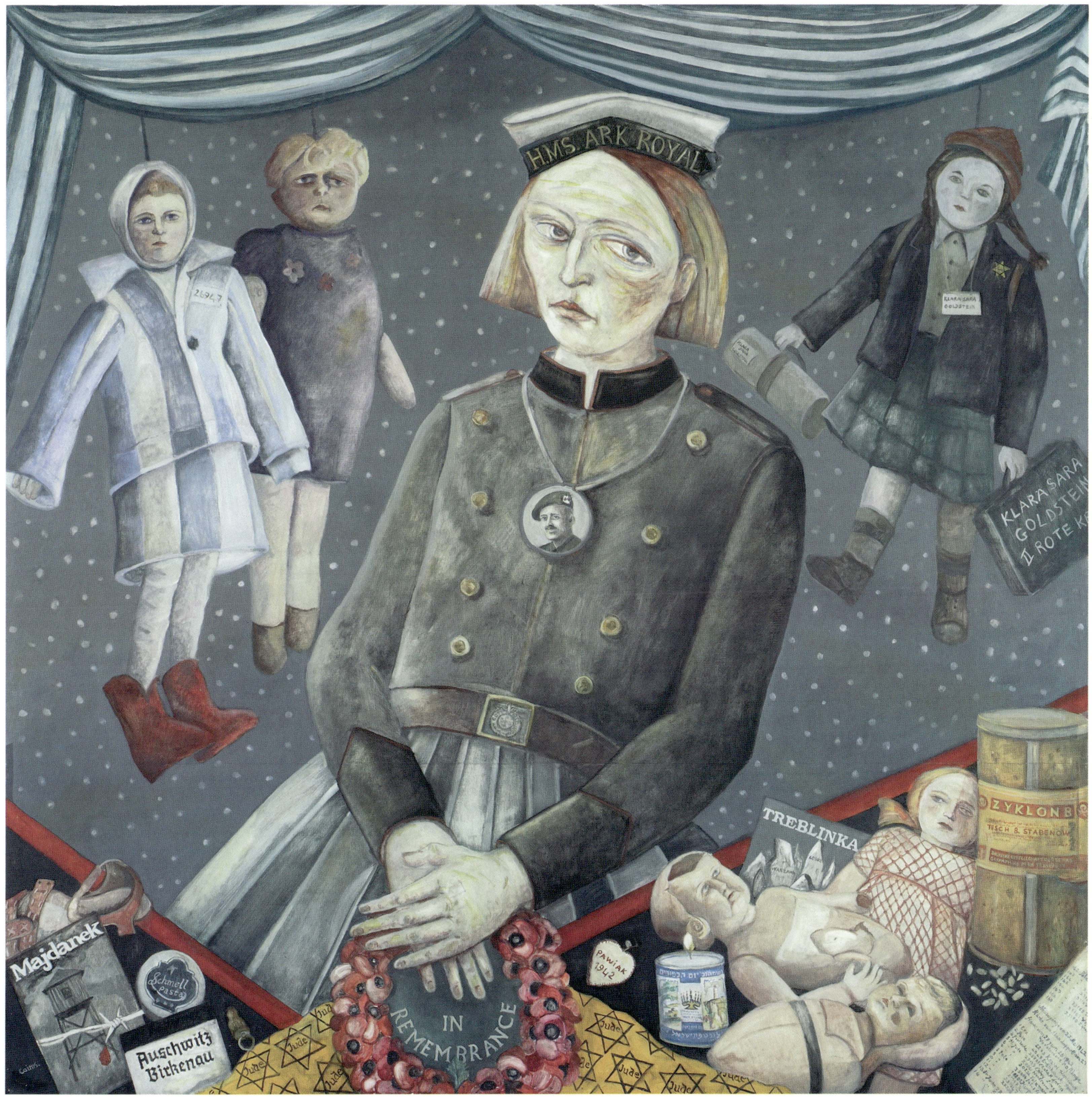
H.M.S. ARK ROYAL
KLARA-SARA GOLDSTEIN
TREBLINKA
ZYKLON B
TESCH & STABENOW
Majdanek
PAWIAK 1942
IN REMEMBRANCE
Auschwitz Birkenau
Jude

PLATE TWENTY–SIX

Auschwitz Memorial, 1999–2003

Oil on panels, 213 x 366 cm

On the long corridor walls, hung up on metal grids, are photographs of the incarcerated victims of all ages. All were registered in detail and given camp numbers which replaced their names and were tattooed on their arms. For identification they were photographed from three angles and many of the photographs appeared to have been taken before the inmates even arrived at the camps, but in each one the victim looks apprehensive and frightened.

On returning, I studied my photographs and decided that the only way I could contribute to giving back status, respect and dignity, while acknowledging the desperate suffering and dehumanisation, was by investing each image with individual care and attention through the medium of portraiture. I have felt guilt that I too have had to put these people through yet another selection, as I could not paint them all. But I now know these chosen faces so intimately that they haunt my dreams.

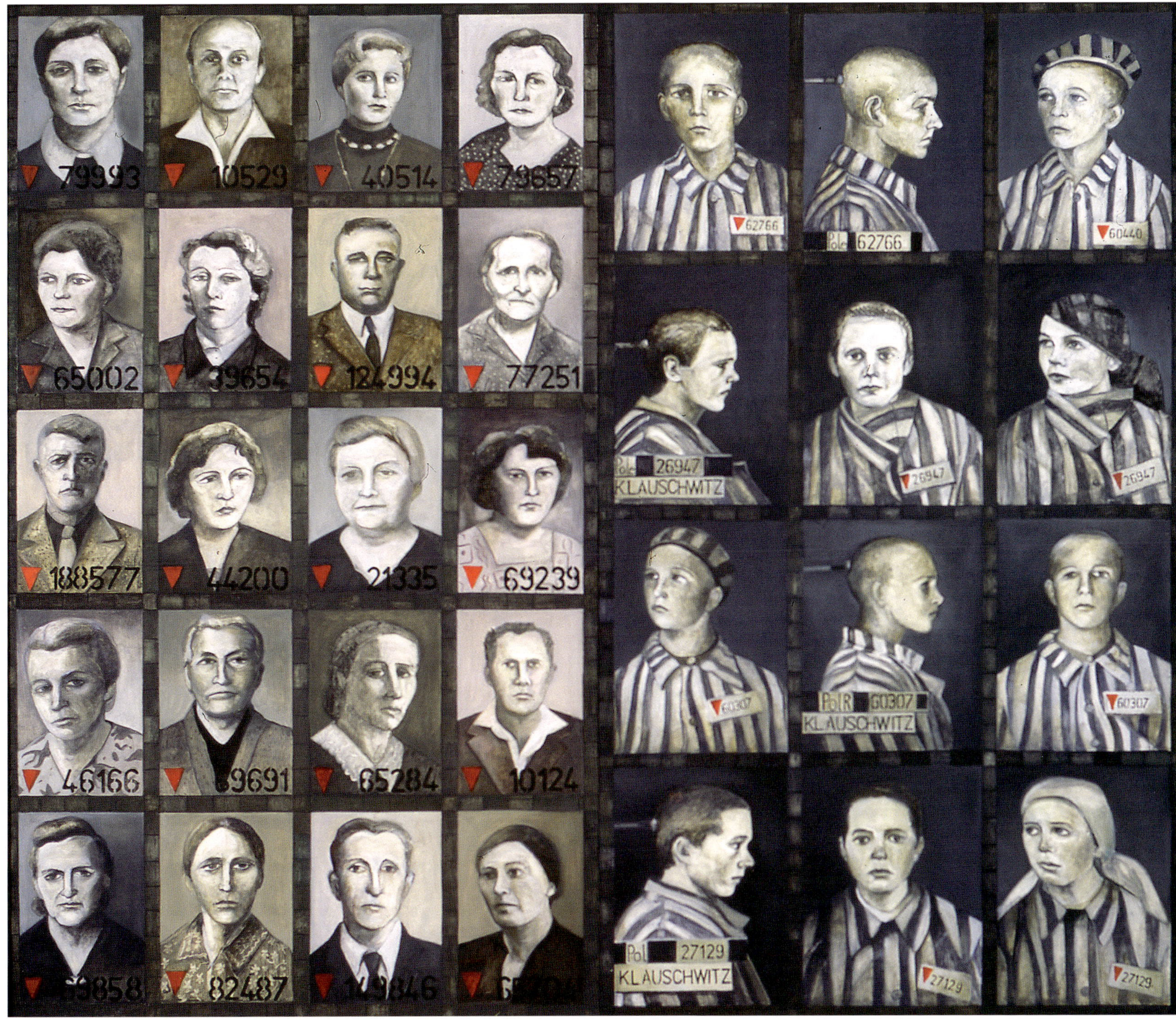
79993
10529
40514
79657
65002
39654
124994
77251
188577
44200
21335
69239
46166
65284
10124
82487
62766
Pole 62766
60440
Pole 26947
KLAUSCHWITZ
26947
26947
60307
PolR 60307
KLAUSCHWITZ
60307
Pol 27129
KLAUSCHWITZ
27129
27129

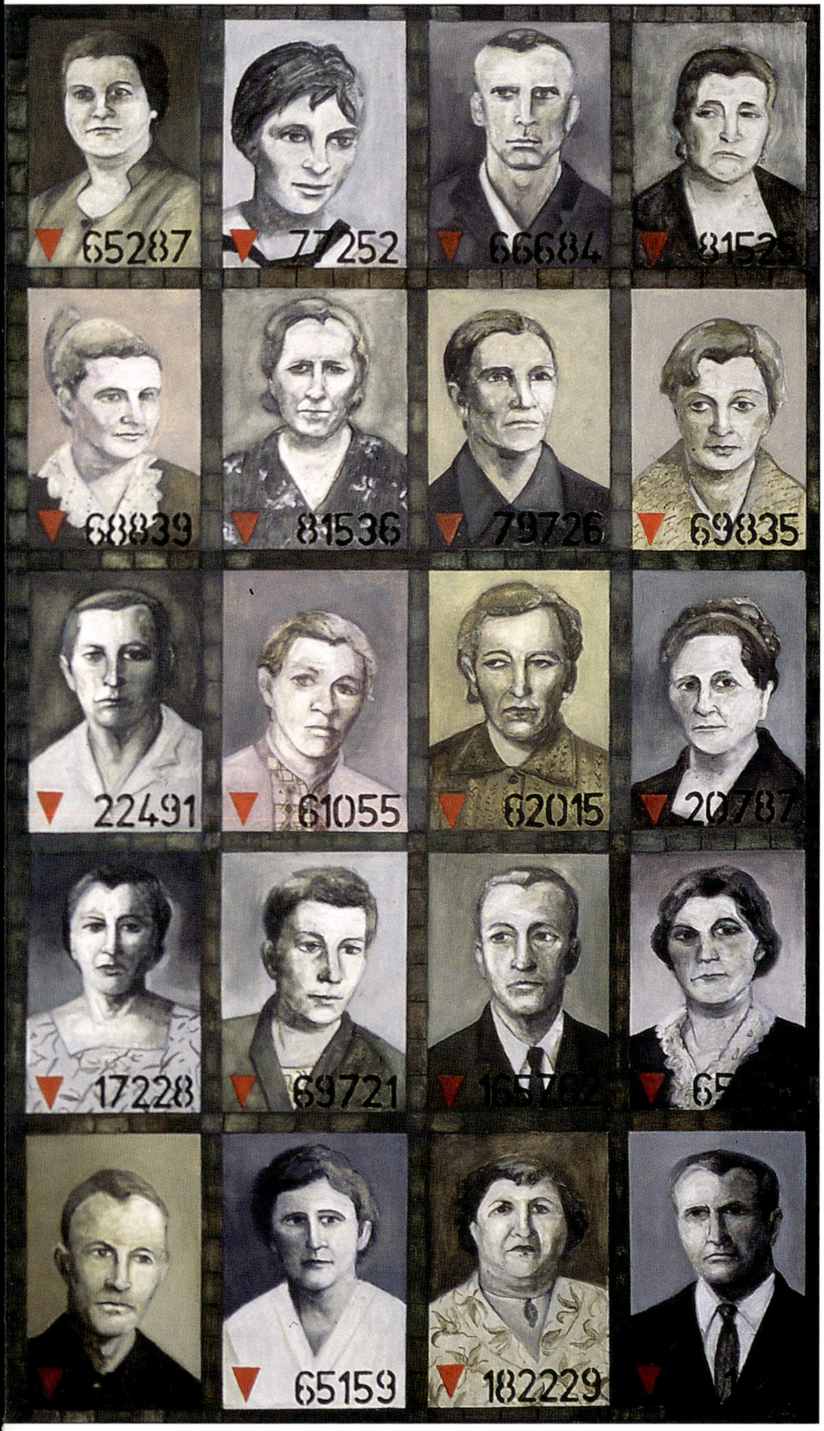

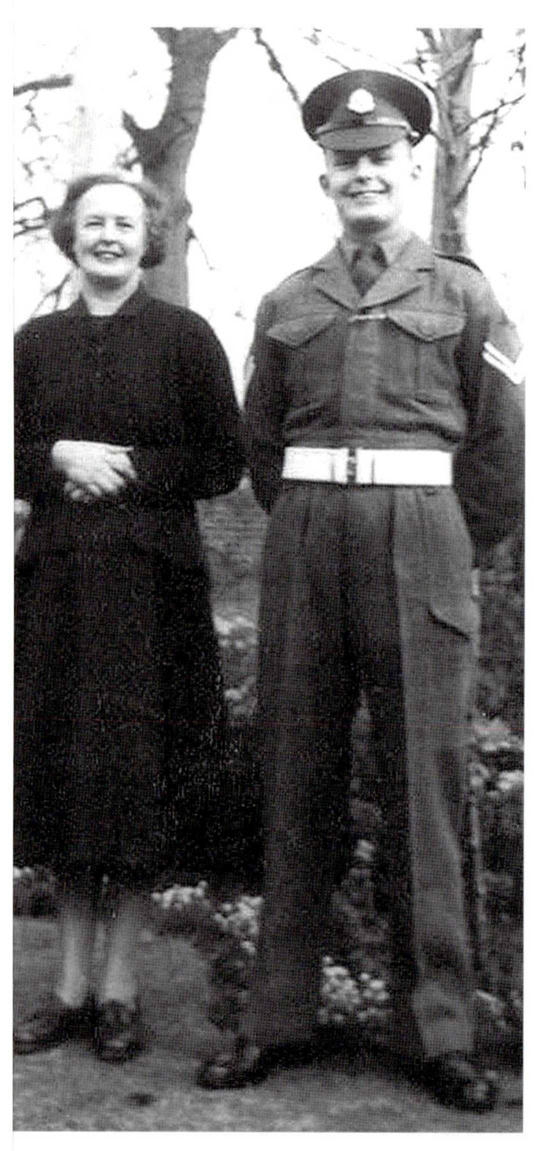

appendix one

A FAMILY STORY

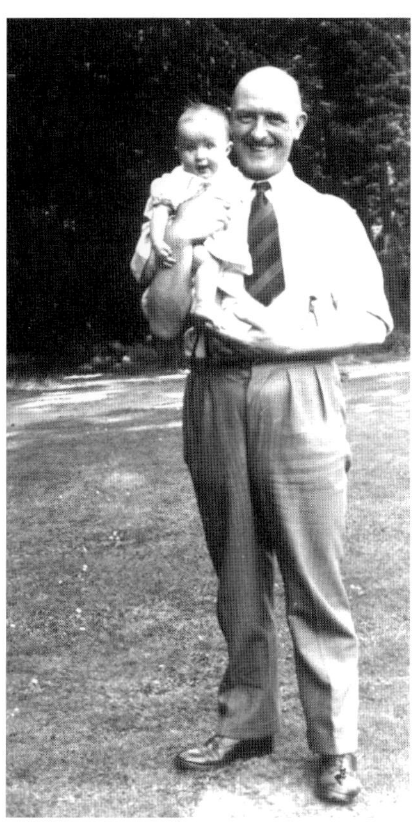

What did you do in the war Daddy?

As far as I remember, this was a question which I never asked.

The fifties and sixties were a time when a generation was trying unsuccessfully to forget the hardships and horrors of war. As a result many families, including my own, were quite dysfunctional. For the fathers of my generation and the one before, in their sleep and after a few drinks, the guilt of surviving the killing, wounding, destruction and suffering often became too much for each individual to bear. There was no counselling, so men tended to come together in clubs and pubs in the evenings where they could pretend for a short time that they were, once again, a band of brothers. Men who had commanded battalions, making life and death decisions, could forget the boredom of a humdrum job in Civvy Street.

The sixties were a time of adolescent indulgence and we had no interest in the sacrifices made by that older generation Men who had survived the Great War, whose eyes were full of painful, dark shadows and whose bodies were frail and often damaged, were still around. Like most girls, I thought my father was a hero. He was funny and full of tales but he was also on many occasions authoritarian and strict. Thrashing was not banned in those days but then one was also belted at school for giving a wrong answer. Just after my first birthday I was given the new triple vaccine which made me very ill and caused many babies to die. Simultaneously I had whooping cough; apparently this same man lay on his old army camp bed by my cot and held my hand for nights on end.

FROM A FAMILY QUESTIONNAIRE:

Do you remember when war was declared and when Dad was called up?

EVELYN: Daddy was always in the TA and we were quite used to seeing him in uniform. I was newly five when war broke out and I expect I heard Mum and Dad talking about it with great anxiety. Dad was called up almost immediately and my first realisation of the war was that on a warm sunny afternoon in September, Dad had gone away. After school Dad appeared in his uniform and all the teachers came round to the school-house, we three children were there. I think they had a glass of sherry and all the teachers said their farewells. One teacher gave Mummy a book and said 'Read this when you go to bed'—it was 'Gone with the Wind'. The book had just been published and the film was being made. I think that helped Mummy a lot.

What was it like in Cawdor during the war—rationing, invasion threats, enemy aircraft?

EVELYN: You ask about rations. Rationing did come in and Daddy told Mum to pack Nancy's pram with all the tins and dried food she could lay

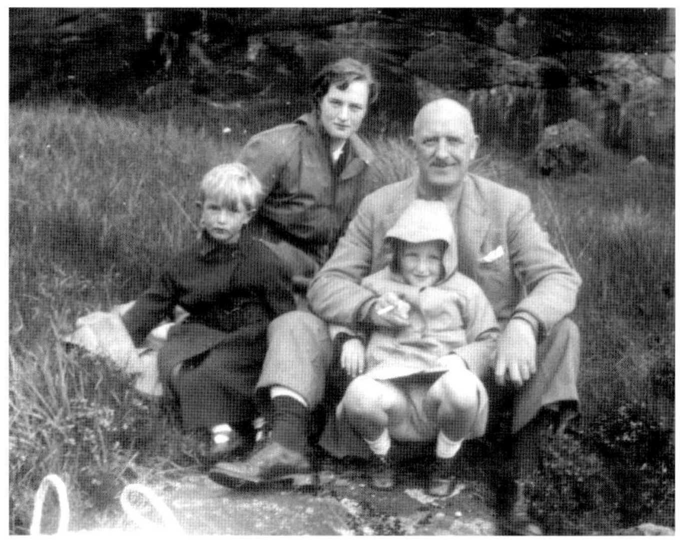

her hands on in case of invasion. He also told her to take us to the woods and go as deep into them as she could. Thankfully we never had to do that. Rationing hit everyone—we used to find a piece of home-made butter in the milk pail or half a dozen eggs, but not very often as everything had to be accounted for.

NANCY: I have two memories—a pram packed with food to be taken into the woods to hide from bad men, and also the Canadian soldiers. I believe they were woodcutters who gave a large party for the school children. We were all given presents and sweets from Santa who wore strange boots and was not like the Santa of my imagination.

Like most women with young children, Mother must have found it very lonely and hard work being on her own. Luckily Father was stationed in Tain for a while and rented an old rambling house where mother and the children joined him. His batman had been a butler in Civvy Street and he still used to serve meals in butler mode. While father was in Tunisia news and letters would have been sporadic and censored.

Father was captured along with two other soldiers and sent to an Italian prisoner of war camp somewhere in Tunisia; it could have been in the foothills of the Atlas Mountains. He was reported as missing. They escaped by garrotting the guards. I was told that he was haunted by the fact that he had killed these Italians in cold blood when they could have been fathers like himself. With the other two soldiers, he escaped by walking over the desert, with no water until they were found by a Catholic priest who hid them in a seminary or monastery. When my father was dying in 1972 the surgeon told him: 'Mr Cairns you have been fighting the Italians throughout the night'. Later, Dad's jeep was blown up by a mine, killing his driver, batman and adjutant. He was thrown over a hedge and was in a coma for four days. He had bits of shrapnel left in his body and I clearly remember the scars on his legs. Tunis fell on 7th May 1943, and in the suitcase with his memorabilia was a rail ticket from Mejez-el-Bab to Tunis for this date. He returned home on compassionate grounds in August because my mother was ill. Dad brought home some dates and told the children that they were camels' eggs, which they had no reason to disbelieve. My brother immediately told his teacher and was given the belt for telling lies.

The family frequently went to Haddington near Edinburgh to stay with an aunt, (Mother's sister) and my grandfather. Finally Mother let the Cawdor schoolhouse and they all moved in with the aunt and grandfather.

This was a very trying time for my mother and she became ill with stress. I do not imagine people were very sympathetic then and one would have been told to pull oneself together, join the war effort and knit some socks.

Do you remember the day Father came home from the war?

EVELYN: We were with Grandfather and Auntie Winnie at Haddington—we had waited all

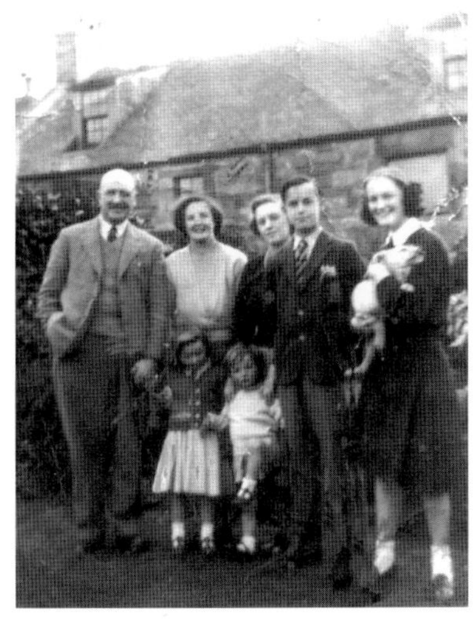

that sunny day and he never appeared. We had no phone so he couldn't contact us. The last train from Edinburgh came into Haddington Station at 9pm. Nancy, Billy and I were meant to be asleep in bed. However when the regular train people came up Haldane Avenue, we three went to the window. Time passed and no one else appeared so we decided to say 'the Lords Prayer' at the end of it we tagged on 'Please send Daddy home.' It was getting dark and suddenly we heard whistling and we just knew it was him and rushed downstairs to the adults who didn't really believe us. But there he was and what a welcome he got. Billy ran and brought Grandfather Dickson's bottle of whisky out of the cupboard. Dad had been held up at the station arranging for his luggage to be brought up the following day.

NANCY (who was only 3 when war broke out): He was a stranger to me but he was called Daddy.

The family went back to Cawdor and Father resumed his duties as headmaster, but he needed more of a challenge. They moved to Edinburgh in 1946 where he took up the appointment as general manager of The Scottish National Camps Association.

I was born in March 1947 and my younger brother followed a year later.

Children born just after the war lived through rationing until 1953; we knew nothing better, so it was not a hardship apart from the lack of sweeties. I remember sugar mice with string tails. A friend of my mother would bring them and in the morning we always knew when she had visited because the string tails hung down over the mantle piece. Families with relatives abroad would often receive parcels of cast-off clothes during this time. We used to get them from South Africa from one of my father's brothers. I received a bright emerald green dirndl skirt with a multi-coloured smocked waistband, which I loved. At Christmas they sent boxes of preserved sugared fruit, which in spite of having no sweets we disliked and there would still be some left when the next box arrived, the following year.

After the war Father continued in the TA but my brother Bill did his National Service in Cyprus during the EOKA troubles.

Photographs from
the War Tours
Archive.

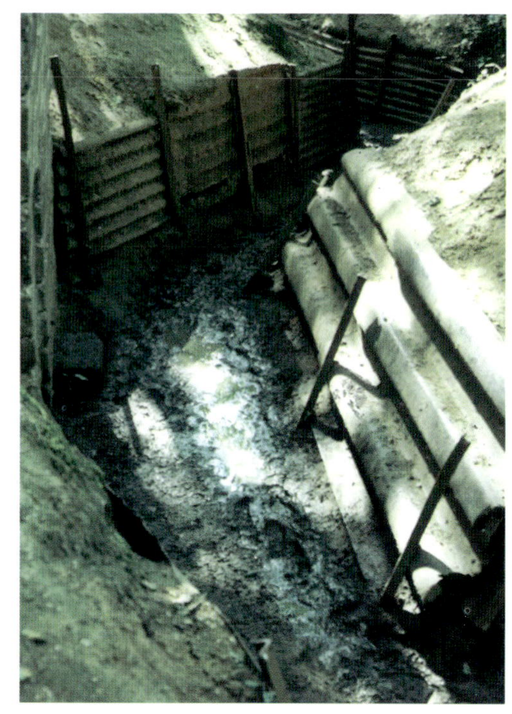

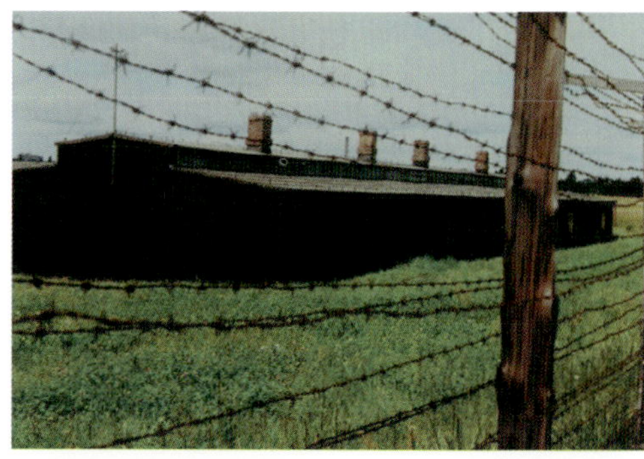

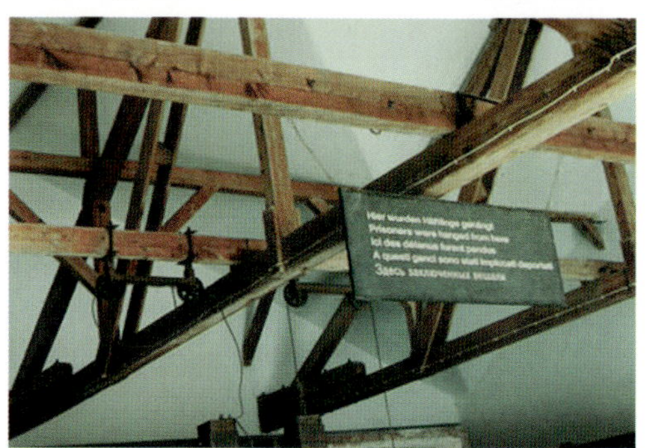

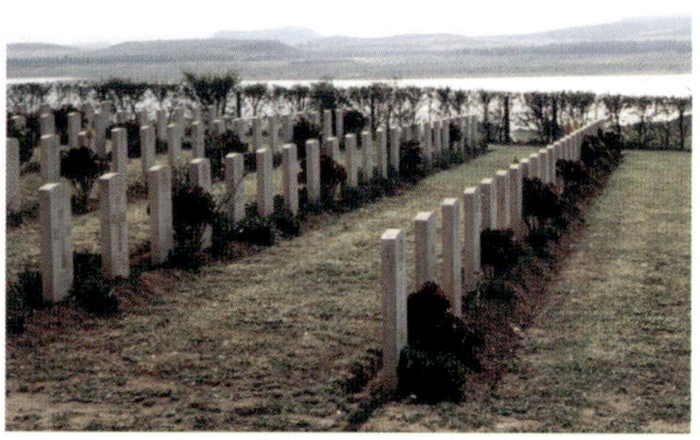

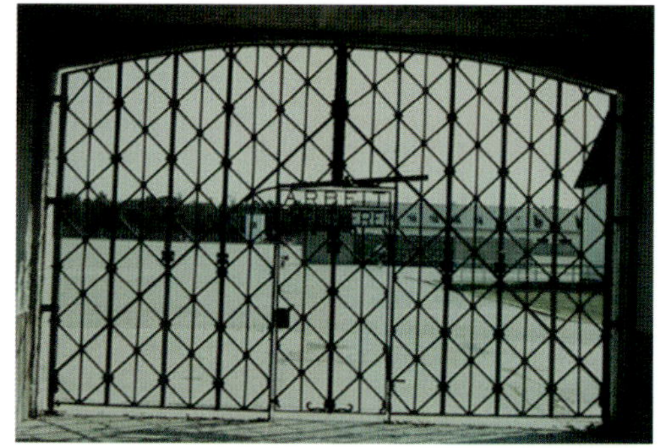

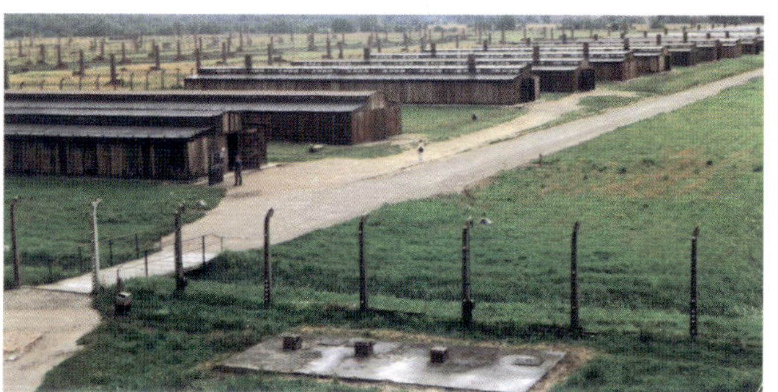

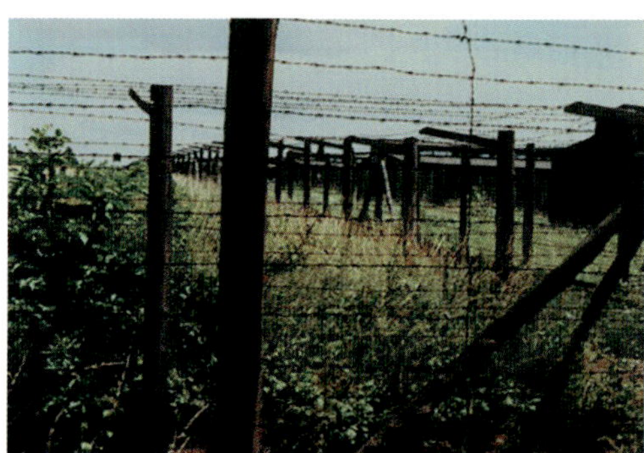

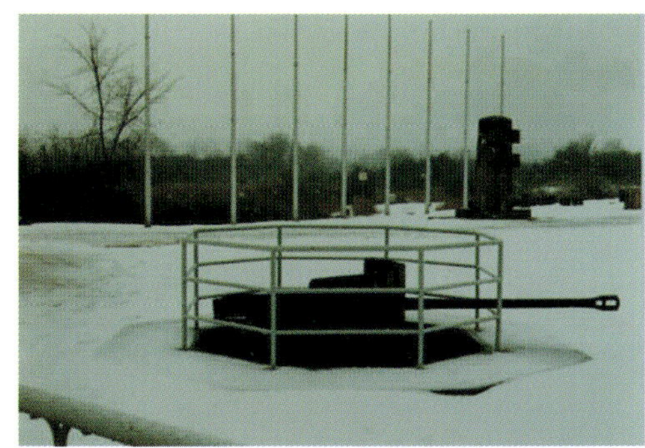

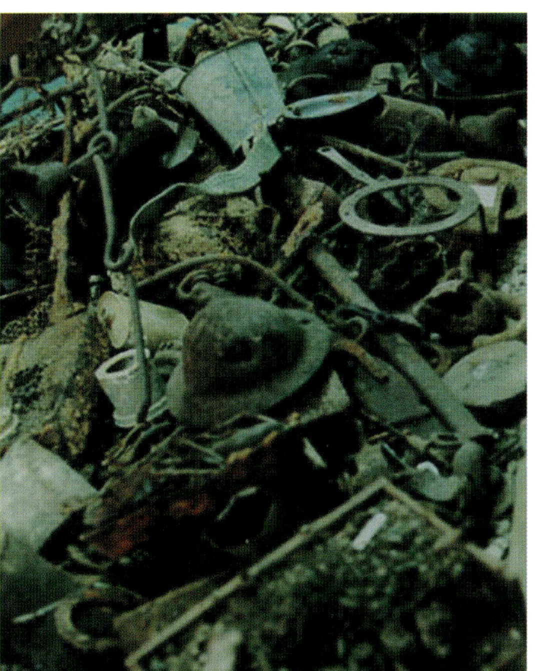

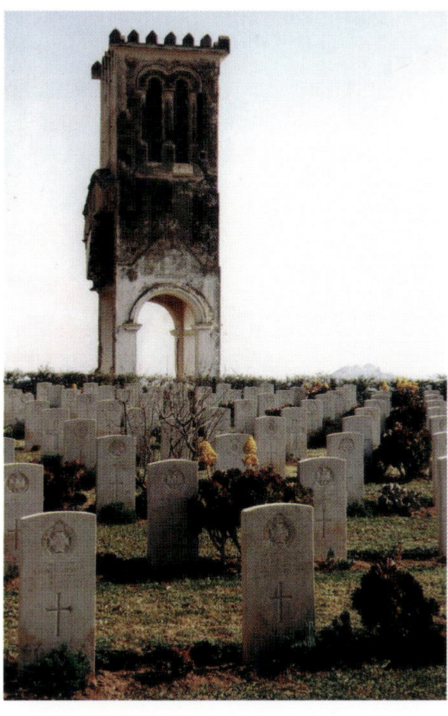

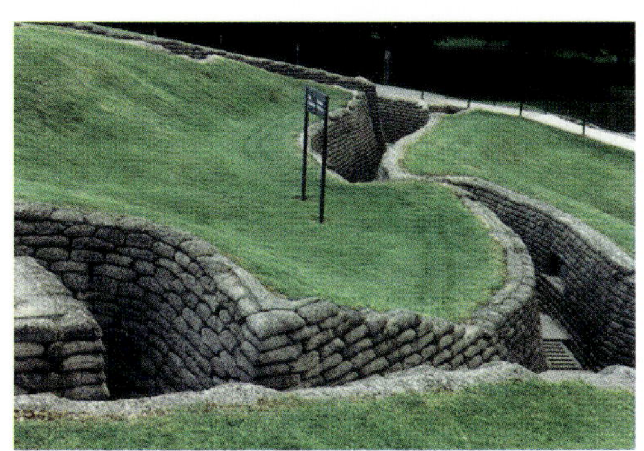

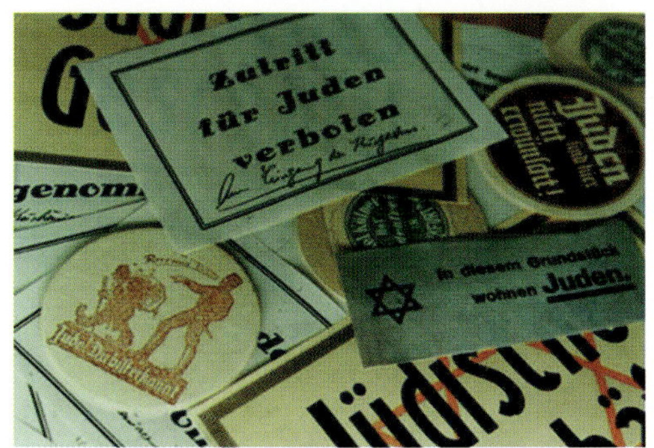
Zutritt
für Juden
verboten
In diesem Grundstück
wohnen Juden.

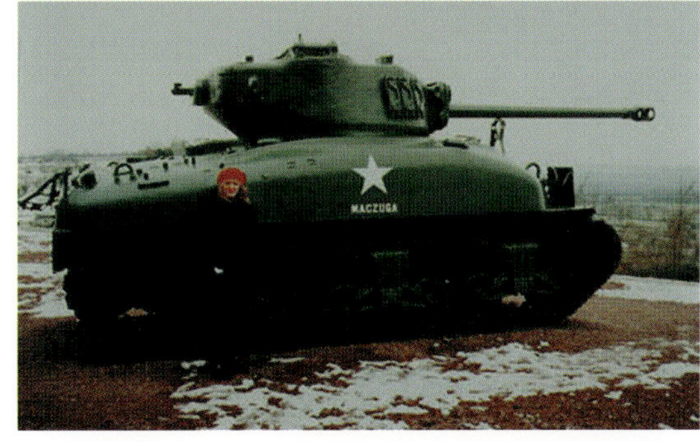
MACZUGA

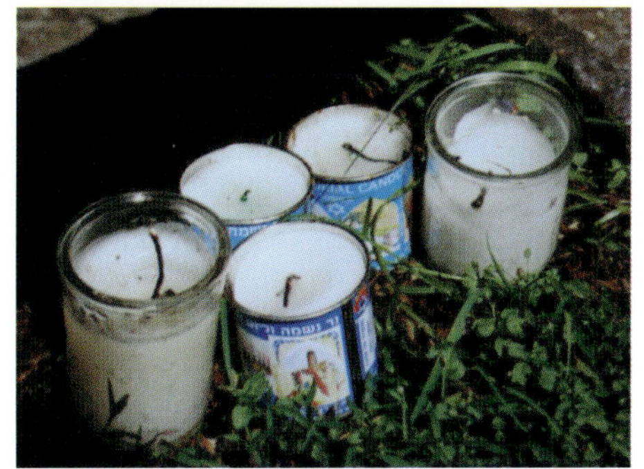

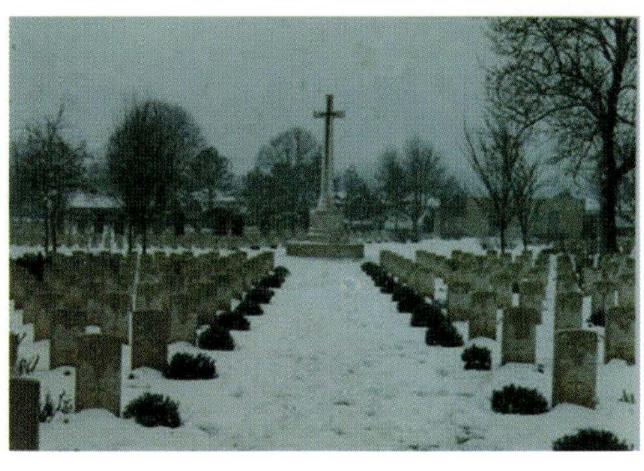

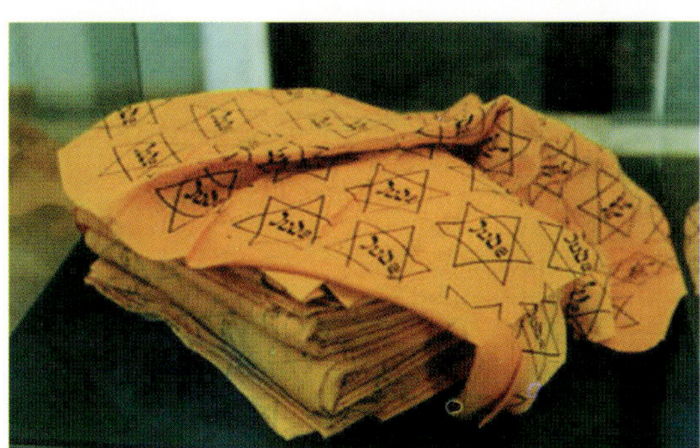

appendix two

EXTRACTS FROM A WAR TOURS DIARY

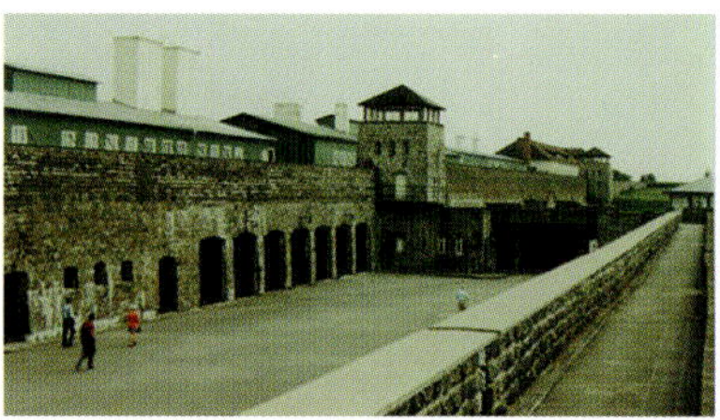

FRIDAY AUGUST 5, 1995:
MAUTHAUSEN

If there is a God, he will have to ask my forgiveness—an inmate at Mauthausen.

This infamous camp sits on a small mountain in the beautiful Austrian countryside of 'The Sound of Music'. The granite fortress was built with the most primitive tools and with bare hands, following Heinrich Himmler's policy of 'death through work' to the letter.

In this place people who were innocent of any crime were tortured to death in the rock quarry .The quarry has one hundred and eighty steep steps to the top which some of us climbed. Prisoners had to carry huge stones to the top and many fell through exhaustion, disease and malnutrition, causing those behind to topple to their death. The guards were known to line up Jewish prisoners at the top and get each to push the one in front to the pool far below. They also experimented with shooting two people with one bullet. Russian prisoners of war, who were regarded as subhuman, were left outside with no shelter, to starve to death. In winter they would take a naked man outside and pour water over him, let him freeze and repeat the process until he was encased in a block of ice.

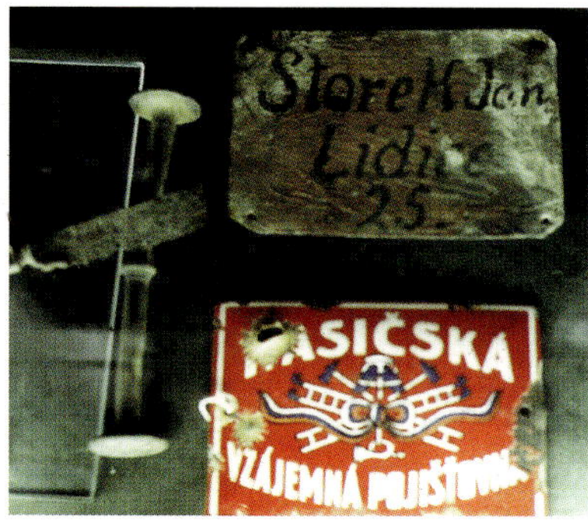

SATURDAY AUGUST 6, 1995:
LIDICE

We visited Lidice in Czecho-slovakia, ten miles from Prague, on a beautiful sunny day and walked through the meadows full of wild flowers. This village was totally destroyed as a retribution for the assassination of Reinhard Heydrich on the June 4, 1942. Five days later German Troops entered the village, imprisoned the women in the school and the men and boys over fifteen in farm buildings. They then ransacked the houses for anything of value; farm tools were taken and cattle rounded up. The women were taken to Ravensbruck Concentration camp and of the ninety-eight children taken from their mothers, only seventeen survived, having been selected for 'Germanisation'. The rest died in Chemnitz.

Seventy-three men and boys were executed in batches against a wall covered in mattresses. The Germans destroyed the village; orchards were dug up, dogs shot and the land ploughed flat. Nothing was left. Today you can see some foundations and a museum housing a few simple artefacts.

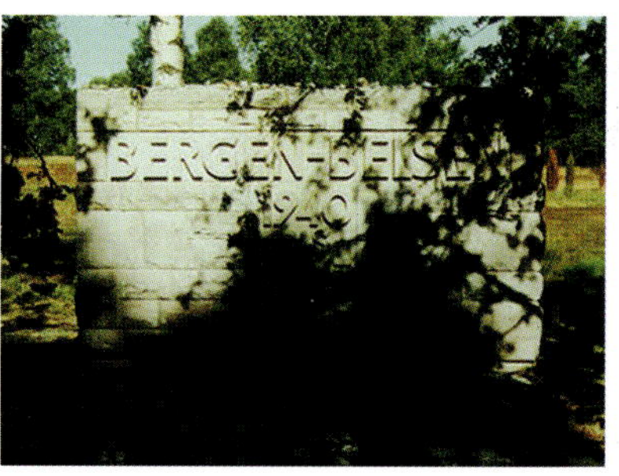

WEDNESDAY AUGUST 10, 1995:
BERGEN-BELSEN

In April 1945 British soldiers liberated Bergen-Belsen. They could not believe the terrible site that met their eyes. Masses of dead, naked and skeletal bodies lying in piles. The living barely alive, lying beside the dead, too weak to move themselves and an epidemic of typhus among the many diseases rife in the camp.

Tony, a fellow traveller and a lovely man, served with The Royal Artillery and landed on D-Day aged eighteen. He was camped outside Bergen-Belsen and said the stench was unbearable. Some of his regiment, because the artillery was no longer needed, had to occupy the camp. They were all horrified and desperately wanted to exact their own justice, but were asked to exercise restraint. Twelve student doctors, only three years into their training, were sent out from St Thomas's in London to help with this dreadful situation. Because of the typhus epidemic, the British burned the camp to the ground and all that remains are the long raised burial mounds surrounded by grassland and trees.

Tony also told me about his father who had served with the Scottish Border Regiment in the First War. On the push from Arras to Cambrai, his father was wounded, losing his lower arm. Two friends were pulling him out the shell hole when both died, shot by a sniper. He stayed down in the hole until it was quieter and managed to heave himself partly out. He was then hit again but the bullet went sideways and was slightly deflected by his wallet that contained a wad of letters and an old watch. Instead of the bullet going into his heart it went through his chest, just clipping the lung and out the other side. He fell back into the hole yet, despite his awful injuries, managed to crawl out again. He was very thirsty and crawled over to a dead officer and took his flask. This contained whisky which he downed, then struggled to the dressing station. The surgeon said it was the whisky that saved his life. He had gangrene so his arm was amputated above the elbow to give him protection. Tony has the wallet and watch with the bullet hole but has no family to whom he could leave them. I suggested he contact The Imperial War Museum.

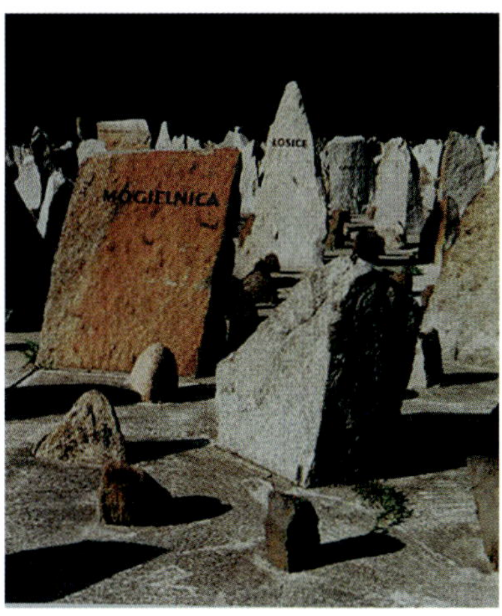

TUESDAY JULY 9, 1997: TREBLINKA

Treblinka, like Belzec and Sobidor was a killing centre, unlike most of the other camps where there was a slim possibility that inmates might, through work, survive the war.

We are very close to the Russian border and have just passed a sign for Minsk. We are driving through a deep, dark forest of tall pine trees, similar to the scene in Dr. Zhivago when he walks through the woods to find the Red Train. All the houses we have passed are squat wooden structures with intricate carved shutters. There are large storks nesting on some of the chimneys—amazing, I've never seen a stork before.

Treblinka was set in these woods to be hidden, with no towns nearby. It was near a railway, essential for transports, and was initially a punitive Labour camp but, in 1941, became a Holocaust factory. Treblinka 2 was built in 1942 by existing prisoners and was surrounded by a three metre high barbed wire fence entwined with branches so that no-one could see inside. A make-believe railway station was built to deceive the incoming trainloads of Jews from all over Europe. There were ten gas chambers where over eight-hundred thousand were murdered. The entire transport—men, women and children, were driven naked, supposedly to the showers. Inside the chamber, victims were made to stand with their arms uplifted, so more could be squeezed in—children were flung on top of this mass. The gassing took fifteen minutes. The bodies were then removed by Jewish workers and layered with wood in an immense grave fed with flammable liquid. This burned day and night and the stench and ashes of the burned bodies covered the whole area. On several occasions up to eighteen thousand victims were burnt daily and very few escaped.

The Germans destroyed the camp in November 1943. It is now a Memorial Field with hundreds of different sizes and colours of hewn rocks, on which are engraved the names of the places from whence the victims came as we walked around, pollen and bits of stuff were falling from the lime trees and seemed like ashes in the wind.

Got back to the hotel at 8.15—what a long and sad day. Up at 6.20 tomorrow. This trip is hard going both mentally and physically.

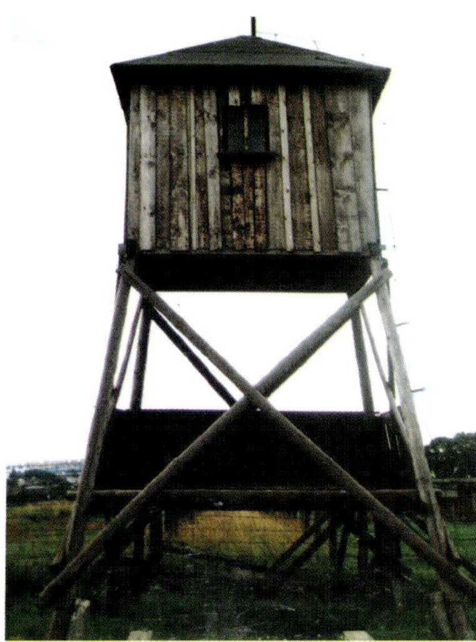

WEDNESDAY JULY 10, 1997: MAJDANEK

En route for Majdanek, via Lublin, for the second largest concentration camp after Auschwitz Birkenau. The countryside is very flat with forests and strip farming.

According to Anya, our Polish guide, during Soviet rule there was a shortage of food and other goods; it all went to Russia but the farmers still made a good living by selling any surplus in the cities. They started building new houses to accommodate three generations and would add upwards and outwards each year; no planning permission is necessary. At the end of Russian rule there was plenty of food and the farmers, without extra income, have been unable to finish their houses so the countryside is littered with these bizarre, incomplete Heath Robinson buildings. The farms themselves are very inefficient. Every time an owner dies the land is split up equally amongst the remaining family which is why the ground is in strips with potatoes, cabbage, beetroot and maize as the main crops. After the war Polish soldiers who fought in the West could not return to their homeland for fear of persecution from the Russians. The Poles themselves murdered many Jewish survivors, who after their liberation, did try to go back to their homes and sadly, to this day, Anti-Semitism still exists in Poland. You do notice how run down, neglected, unprosperous and quiet some of the towns are, especially in the former Jewish neighbourhoods. Before the war these towns were vibrant with activity, commerce and cultural events and might have remained so if the mass killing had not occurred.

We have just arrived at Majdanek. It is a vast camp, just off the main road and terrifying to see, with primitive wooden huts and watch towers stretching out before us.

In winter, the temperature falls well below freezing and the areas between the blocks became frozen mud. Roll calls held here could last for up to fourteen hours and hundreds died of exposure. The camp contains the largest crematorium I have seen; a group of third generation Israeli Jews plus a couple of older men who appeared to be camp survivors, holding a service and putting lit candles in the ovens. The plaintive songs and chants made me cry.

One of the grimmest days in Majdanek occurred in November 1943, when an estimated 18,400 Jews were killed. In batches they were stripped, whipped and savaged by dogs then pushed into deep ditches and machine-gunned one layer on top of the next. Jazz music was played from loud speakers to drown out the screams.

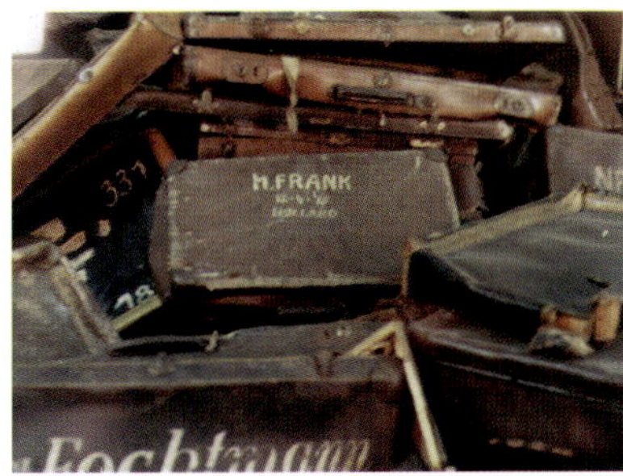

SUNDAY JULY 13, 1997: AUSCHWITZ

7.30am, on our way out of Cracow, having been up at 6am. Some of us, as usual, have sneaked a little extra from the breakfast table, as from experience. there are unlikely to be any service stations en route. Brian reads the riot act over this behaviour and to punish us has put on a rousing Welsh choir singing—'His soul keeps marching on'. Welsh John from somewhere unpronounceable, who sits in front of me is singing along to the music. I just wish it would stop. I think we are all feeling apprehensive about our visit to Auschwitz and Birkenau because of their well-publicised notoriety.

During the war all signposts were changed to German so that the human transports did not know where they were.

On arrival it looks like a major tourist venue, many coaches are parked near the entrance, and hordes of people have arrived by train. As we pass through the gates of the camp we see above them, ARBEIT MACHT FREI (Work makes you free), a painful irony since everything in the camp served death. First impressions—it does not look as frightening and basic as other camps, due to the substantial red brick barracks and the smart walkways and trees. However it has the same history of brutality as all the others.

The SS, with Dr Mengele in attendance, made the selections outside the camp at the railway station, separating those who looked strong enough to be worked to death from the elderly, sick and infirm, the mothers and children, excepting twins and others who were designated for medical experiments.

The blocks all have specialist exhibitions ranging from rooms full of suitcases on which the victims had written their names and addresses, spectacles, hair of all colours, pots and pans from family kitchens and shoes. There is a shocking display of artificial limbs and orthopaedic devices from the disabled, some of which would have belonged to veterans of the Great War

The camp was a vast reservoir of cheap labour and major German companies paid huge sums to the SS to 'rent' the inmates. The camp authorities of course exploited this labour to the maximum, but at the same time destroyed them through starvation and appalling living conditions. Hunger, inadequate sanitation and hygiene, lack of proper clothes and medicines and unbearable workloads killed many. Others were beaten, torn apart by dogs, hanged, shot or given lethal injections for no apparent crime.

In the building dedicated to the memory of Jewish suffering we met the same Israeli group from Madjanek, holding a service over a pit in the floor containing bone relics.

In 1940 Auschwitz was expanded into three main camps: Auschwitz I, Auschwitz II-Birkenau and Auschwitz III-Monowitz, in addition there were more than forty smaller camps. I must admit that before I visited Dachau I had not realised the existence of these peripheral camps.

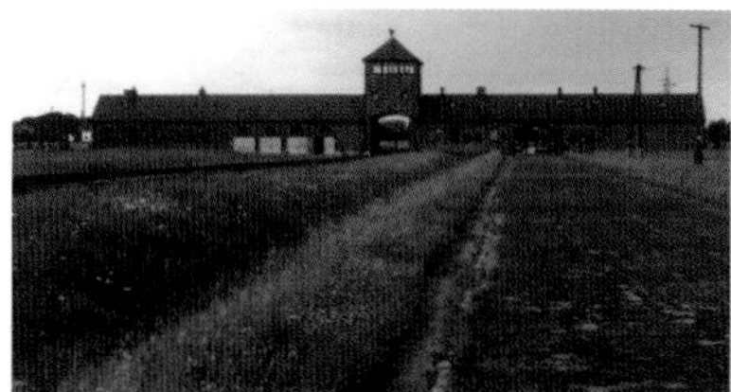

SUNDAY JULY 13, 1997: BIRKENAU:

Rudolph Höss, the camp commandant, was given the job of expanding the camp and this annexe was supposedly capable of housing a hundred thousand prisoners.

We started from the far end of the camp and walked back, firstly through a copse of birch trees where the prisoners had to wait after alighting from the trains and before they were taken to the gas chambers. Beyond that is the field of ashes where there are some large wooden Stars of David stuck in the ground. Unlike Auschwitz, Birkenau is a vast space, nearly a mile square, and is almost deserted. In another field we found a large pile of prisoners' effects, rusting cutlery, metal bowls and fragments of shoes lying on the ground covered by a metal grid. Welsh John handed me a shoelace that he said was sticking out of the pile.

When the end of the war was approaching, the SS attempted to remove all evidence of the atrocities committed. They dismantled and dynamited the four gas chambers, and destroyed the crematoria and other buildings. Substantial remains are still there. They also burnt documents and, as at other camps, evacuated most of the remaining prisoners who were capable of walking. They were sent on 'Death Marches' with little or no food or water, inadequate clothing and wooden clogs, towards the interior of the Reich. When they collapsed and could go no further, they were shot. More Jews, including those from Auschwitz, were killed in Birkenau than anywhere else. The huts foundations and brick chimneystacks still stand earily, covering a huge area. The actual huts were burnt down, but some of the few remaining contain the three-tiered bunks, on which six prisoners slept, usually without even a straw pallet.

Conditions were shocking. The ground was thick with mud in which the prisoners had to stand, for hours on end at roll-call. If it rained, prisoners lay all night in their soaked clothes. Toilet blocks for both sexes were just rows of holes in a concrete shelf and there was little water for washing.

While we were walking around it was very overcast and there was a thunder and lightning storm which made the whole place seem even more horrific. We eventually arrived at the infamous main gate and guard post, 'The Gate of Death' through which the railway track runs to the death installations.

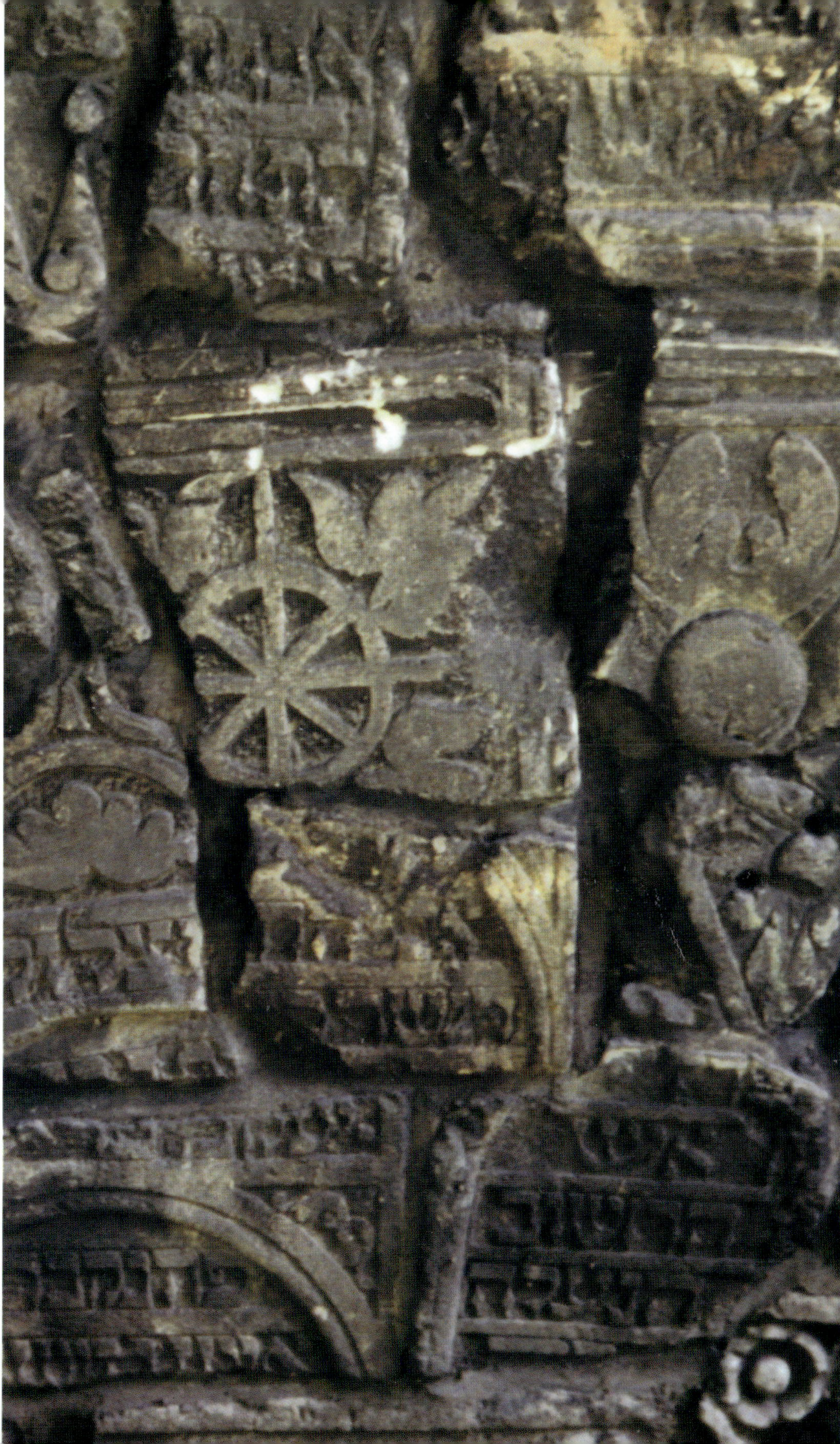

SELECTED BIBLIOGRAPHY, JOYCE CAIRNS' TEXTS

Atkinson, R.
An Army at Dawn, The War in North Africa 1942-43, Abacus, 2004

Battlefield Review, Issue No 1, Wharncliffe Publishing Ltd

Coombs, R.E.B.
Before Endeavours Fade, A Guide to the Battlefields of the First World War, Battle of Britain Prints International, 1999

Delaforce, P.
Monty's Ironsides, From the Normandy Beaches to Bremen with the Third Division, Chancellor Press, 1995

Finel, G. and F.
Remember 44, Editions Ouest-France, 1994

Gardiner, J.
The 1940's House, Channel 4 Books, 2002

Gilbert, M.
Holocaust Journey, Weidenfeld & Nicolson, The Orion Publishing Group, 1997

Giles, J.
Flanders Then and Now, The Ypres Salient and Passchendaele, Heronsgate Ltd, 1987

Healey, T.
Life on the Home Front, Reader's Digest Association Ltd, 1994

Marszatek, J.
Majdanek, The concentration camp in Lubin, Interpress, Warsaw, 1986

Moorehead, A.
African Trilogy, The North African Campaign 1940-1943, Cassel, 1998

Opie, R.
The 1910's Scrapbook, The Decade of the Great War, New Cavendish Books

Poems of the Great War 1914-1918, Penguin Books, 1998

Rogerson, B. and Baring, R.
Cadogan Guides: Tunisia, Cadogan Books Ltd, 1992

Scheel, Dr. W. (ed.)
Bergen-Belsen—Explanatory Notes on the Exhibition, Niedersachsische Landeszentrale für Politische Bildung, Hannover, 1991

Swiebocki, T. and H.
Auschwitz, Voices from the Ground, Panstwowe Muzeum, Oswiecim-Brzezinka, Parol Ltd

Treblinka Muzeum, Walki I Meczenstwa w. Treblince, 1996

ADDITIONAL BIBLIOGRAPHIES OR FOOTNOTES:

Bill Hare, p.24
Stuart Allan, p.39
Sandy Moffat, p.49

BIOGRAPHIES

JENNIFER MELVILLE has been Keeper of Fine Art at Aberdeen Art Gallery since 1995. She received her degree in the History of Art from Aberdeen University and followed this with further study at Manchester University. She completed a PhD at the University of Edinburgh in 2000. Her research interests lie mainly in the area of late 19th century art.

BILL HARE was educated at Southport Art College, University of Edinburgh and the Courtauld Institute, University of London. He worked as Exhibition Organiser at the Talbot Rice Gallery, Edinburgh, where he put on major national and international exhibitions, mainly concentrating on modern and contemporary Scottish art. He now teaches as lecturer, in the Centre for Visual and Cultural Studies at Edinburgh College of Art and as an Honorary Fellow in the department of Art History at the University of Edinburgh. He has published extensively on Scottish art and is the author of *Contemporary Painting in Scotland*.

STUART ALLAN is Senior Curator of Military History at the National Museums of Scotland, based at the National War Museum in Edinburgh Castle. After spells on the staff of the Gordon Highlanders' Museum and Aberdeen Art Gallery, he remains fondly attached to Aberdeen and its nearby mountains. His latest publication is *The Thin Red Line: war, empire and visions of Scotland* (NMS Enterprises).

ALEXANDER MOFFAT was born in Dunfermline in 1943 and studied painting at Edinburgh College of Art. From 1968–78 he was Chairman of the New 57 Gallery, Edinburgh.
In 1979 he joined the staff of the Glasgow School of Art where he was Head of Painting until his retirement in 2005. The Third Eye Centre, Glasgow, organised a travelling exhibition (1981–83) of his portraits of Scottish poets. He has written extensively on Scottish art and has selected several important exhibitions of contemporary painting. Alexander Moffat was awarded an OBE in the recent New Year's Honours List.

ARTHUR WATSON trained at Gray's of Art in Aberdeen where he founded Peacock Printmakers in 1974. He is now Senior Lecturer in Fine Art at the University of Dundee and is part of a team carrying out research in the Demarco Archives. He represented Scotland at the Venice Biennale in 2000 and currently sculptural projects are in progress on Skye and Cairn Gorm and in East Lothian.

DONALD ADDISON, born 1937 in Glasgow, is a chartered designer. Formerly on the staff at Gray's School of Art and a president of Aberdeen Artists' Society, he ran a design and small publishing business. He is a practising printmaker with an interest in the palliative role of the visual arts in hospitals and hospices.

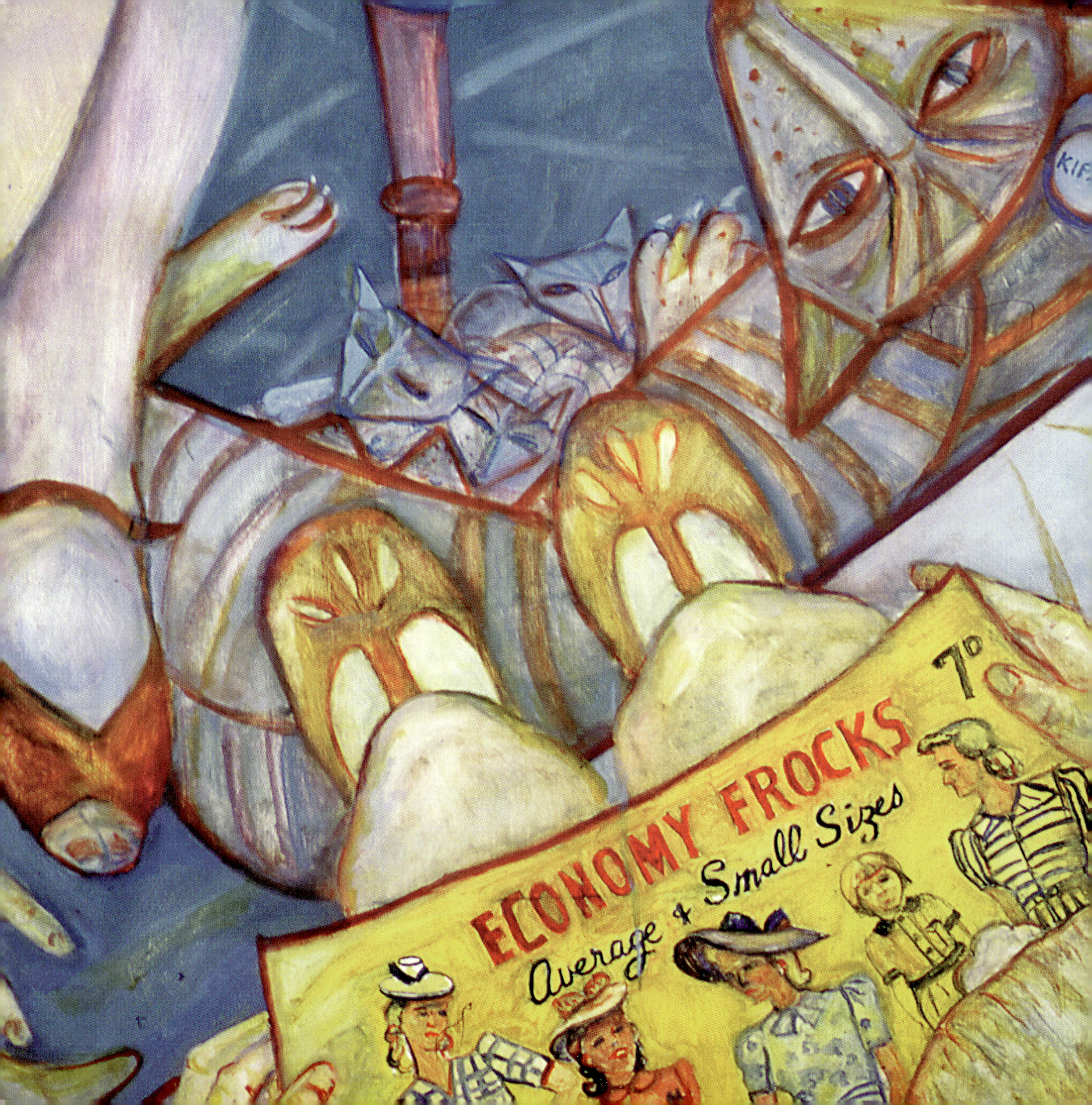
7D
ECONOMY FROCKS
Average & Small Sizes

ARTIST'S ACKNOWLEDGEMENTS

I would like to thank DEIRDRE GRANT and the STAFF of ABERDEEN ART GALLERY for their commitment to the development and presentation of the exhibition that accompanies this book and to the SCOTTISH ARTS COUNCIL NATIONAL LOTTERY FUND for their support of the exhibition as a whole and its educational and interpretative activities.

For kindly loaning paintings from their collections I am grateful to:
HIGHLAND COUNCIL,
THE CITY OF EDINBURGH MUSEUMS AND GALLERIES,
PERTH AND KINROSS COUNCIL,
ABERDEEN ASSET MANAGEMENT PLC and
THE ROYAL SCOTTISH ACADEMY

I acknowledge financial assistance from THE ROBERT GORDON UNIVERSITY, through their RESEARCH COMMITTEE, to the initial research essential to the preparation of many of the paintings illustrated in this book and to THE GILLIES COMMITTEE OF THE ROYAL SCOTTISH ACADEMY for a bursary enabling extensive travel in Eastern Europe.

I would like to express my grateful thanks to ABERDEEN ASSET MANAGEMENT PLC for their generous sponsorship of this publication, to THE CARNEGIE TRUST FOR THE UNIVERSITIES OF SCOTLAND for a grant towards colour illustrations, to the quartet of writers who provided illuminating and insightful responses to the work and its context: JENNIFER MELVILLE, STUART ALLAN, BILL HARE and ALEXANDER MOFFAT, to STUART JOHNSTONE for once again photographing my paintings with sensitivity and of course to DONALD ADDISON and ARTHUR WATSON for their help and guidance for the graphic coherence that they have brought to this publication, also to ANDY RICE for the design and production of the multi-media projection which adds further depth to the exhibition.

Finally I would like to thank my dear friends EDI STARK and DUANE MEAD for their sympathetic support during my tribulations in preparing for this exhibition and to my long-suffering husband ROBERT who, as well as driving round battlefield sites in Tunisia, Normandy and The Western Front, has had to cope with my stress, anxiety and neglect of housekeeping.

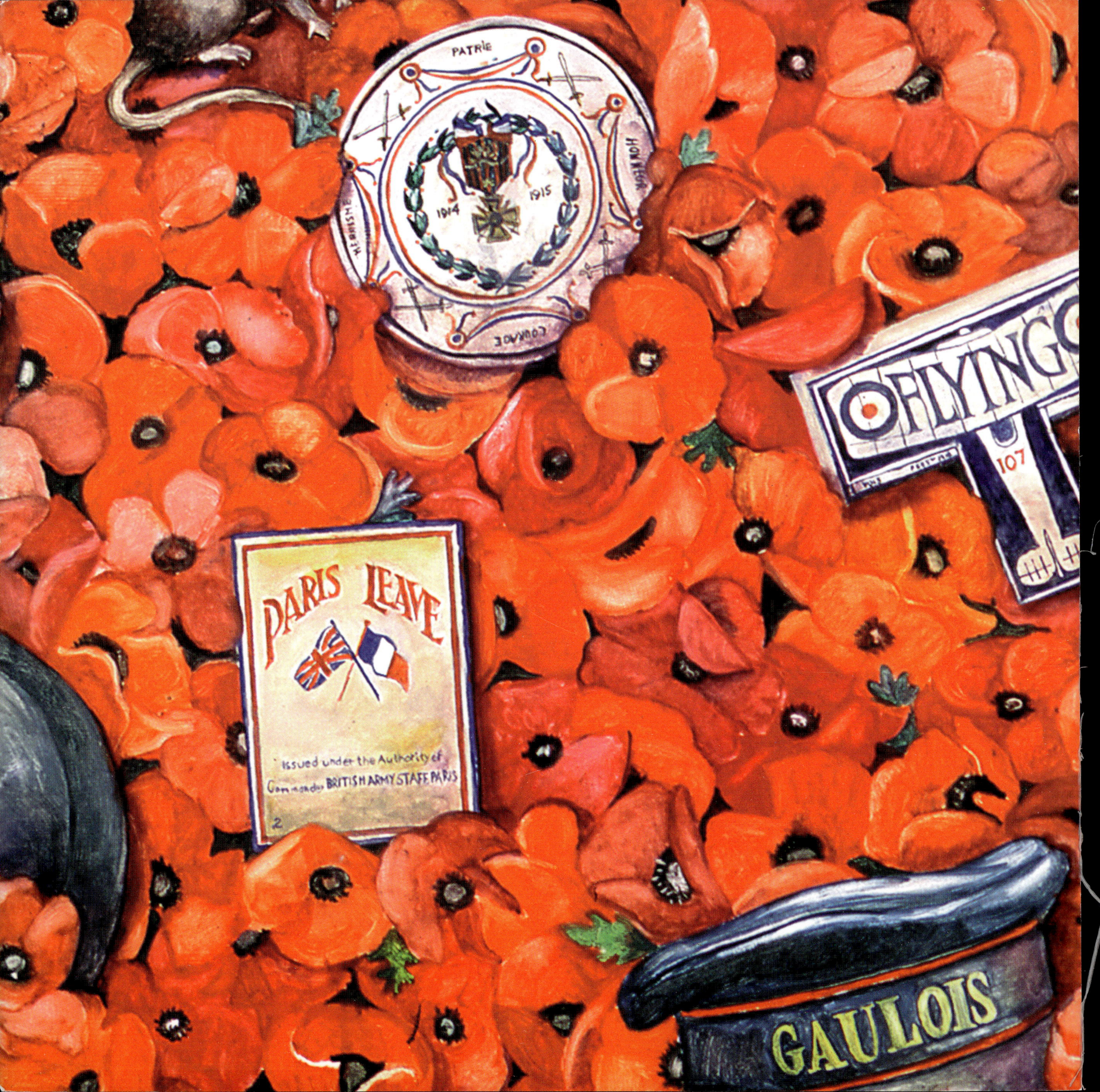
PATRIE
HONNEUR
COURAGE
1914
1915
PARIS LEAVE
Issued under the Authority of
BRITISH ARMY STAFF PARIS
2
107
GAULOIS